Time with
The Timeless One

Lisa Buffaloe

Time with The Timeless One

Copyright 2019 Lisa Buffaloe (Updated 7/12/23)
John 15:11 Publications, Florence, AL 35630

All rights reserved. No part of this book may be reproduced or transmitted in any way, form, or by any means, electronic or mechanical—including photocopying, recording, or by any information storage and retrieval system— except brief quotations in printed reviews. without permission of the author.

Visit the author's website at https://lisabuffaloe.com

ISBN-13: 978-1-7335608-0-1
ISBN-10: 1-7335608-0-7

Cover photo: Dennis Buffaloe
Cover design: Lisa Buffaloe

Printed in the United States of America

I write *"not for professional theologians but for plain persons whose hearts stir them up to seek after God Himself."* ~ A. W. Tozer

Timeless

Time is something I desire to better manage, but time is ... well ... pretty unmanageable. When younger, I couldn't wait for time to hurry so I'd be old enough to do things on my own. Now I'm older and have time to do things on my own, yet time seems to race past only leaving me more tired and wrinkled.

The more time I try to squeeze out of life, the more time squeezes through my life.

I want time to speed through the bad things and pause to enjoy the good things. If only I could use time wisely, live fully in the moment, and not worry about the time to come, time would no longer be a friend or foe, but merely a vehicle to travel through time to eternity.

I wish I could tell you I have this time management skill perfected. Unfortunately, I can't. However, I am learning that the best time is time spent with God. When I pull away to draw into God's presence, time seems to stop and yet multiply. The more time given to God, the more time seems to be received.

The moments I have spent in prayer and Bible study, the greater my peace, encouragement, and soul-filling. When I have rested in God's presence, the more rest my soul and body have received.

God is the timeless one. He is the Alpha and the Omega, the Beginning and the End, existing forever. God invites us to come to Him, come into His presence, to be still and know that He is a loving God.

God longs to be part of our lives through every day and moment.

Every time we turn to God, focus on Him, we are gifted with His comfort, peace, joy, wisdom, guidance, and unfailing love. There is no better time than to spend time with the Timeless One.

The devotions in this book are written to bring encouragement, hope, joy, comfort, and especially to help you linger in the timeless truths given throughout the Bible. Come aside and spend time with The Timeless One.

Heavenly Father, thank You that there is an appointed time for everything and a time for every event under heaven. Remind me how brief my time is here on earth and to trust You in all times. Help me to truly live in each moment You have given.

God, thank You that You are a stronghold in time of trouble, and at the end of my earthly time, You will be there to wipe away every tear and fill me with Your eternal peace and joy forever.

God's Timeless Truth

God "is the Alpha and the Omega [the Beginning and the End], [existing forever] and Who was [continually existing in the past] and Who is to come, the Almighty [the Omnipotent, the Ruler of all]" (Revelation 1:8, AMP).

"There is an appointed time for everything. And there is a time for every event under heaven "(Ecclesiastes 3:1, NASB).

"Trust in, lean on, rely on, and have confidence in Him at all times, you people; pour out your hearts before Him. God is a refuge for us (a fortress and a high tower). Selah [pause, and calmly think of that]!" (Psalm 62:8, AMPC).

"The Lord also will be a stronghold for the oppressed, a stronghold in times of trouble" (Psalm 9:9, NASB).

"Now to Him who is able to protect you from stumbling and to make you stand in the presence of His glory, blameless and with great joy, to the only God our Savior, through Jesus Christ our Lord, be glory, majesty, power, and authority before all time, now and forever. Amen" (Jude 24-25, HCSB).

The love you are looking for, longing for

Searching, wanting, longing for love, desperation that beats for the empty places to be filled, for your moaning heart to be complete with love.

We've all been there. All of us have longed to find the one who will be with us through the changes and craziness of life; who will love us no matter what happens; who will love us for who we are.

Oh, friend, I have good news. There is One. There is One who loves you, who loves with an unfailing love, who loves through the good, bad, and ugly of your life. Jesus Christ will never leave you or forsake you. His love is everlasting. His love is like no other. He will never tire of you. His love will never let go.

You are never too old, never too young, never too fat or too thin, too quiet or too loud, or too needy. God's love is steadfast and unchanging. His love always thinks the best of you. His love is deep, wide, high, perfect, and pure.

Jesus tenderly beckons, "Come to Me ... and I will give rest" (Matthew 11:28). Christ Jesus wants to save you; save you from sin and save you for eternity so that you will eternally live in His love. Jesus died and rose again so that your heart would be filled with His eternal love. He gives rest for your heart, mind, and soul. He gives safety and eternal security.

Your heart is home with Jesus. You will never be alone.

When you can't sleep, Jesus will be with you. When you are in the hardships of life, He will be with you.

When your heart is hurting, He will be with you. When you are rejoicing, He will be with you.

When you need a friend, He is always with you. Jesus will be with you throughout your life, always with you, and always for your best. He is peace. He is with you 24/7 and never tires of being with you. He is The Way who gently guides and leads you in the way you should go. He won't ever lie to you. He'll give you the wisdom you need. He is truth and He is life for your body, soul, mind, and heart.

Remember always, God's steadfast love never ceases; His mercies are new every morning and never come to an end.

Looking for love? Longing for love? No greater love, and no other love, will love like Jesus.

Jesus, thank You for Your amazing, grace-filled, wonderful love. Thank You that Your love never ceases, Your love is unfailing, and You are always here with me. Thank You that You are the love that fills every empty place of my heart and soul.

God's Timeless Truth

"Come to Me, all who are weary and heavy-laden, and I will give you rest.... I am gentle and humble in heart, and you will find rest for your souls." (Matthew 11:28-29, NASB).

"I have loved you just as the Father has loved Me; remain in My love [and do not doubt My love for you]." For, "I have loved you with an everlasting love" (John 15:9, AMP), Jeremiah 31:3, Lamentations 3:22-23.

Finding His pleasure

I want a Holy excitement to do all God has desired me to accomplish. I want the joy of living a creative life for a creative, Creator God. I want to pursue God, live for God in the joy of God.

Christian missionary and Olympic Gold medalist, Eric Liddell understood this concept.

> *"I believe God made me for a purpose, but He also made me fast. And when I run, I feel His pleasure."* ~ Eric Liddell

Each of us has an individual race, and when we stay in our lane, we find a sweet spot of moving in tandem with our Creator. When we keep our eyes on the finish line where our Savior waits, that is where we find the most pleasure and we find His pleasure.

A holy excitement comes when we realize we **are** created for a purpose for God's pleasure. "For it is [not your strength, but it is] God who is effectively at work in you, both to will and to work [that is, strengthening, energizing, and creating in you the longing and the ability to fulfill your purpose] for His good pleasure" (Philippians 2:13, AMP).

The Bible tells us to serve the Lord with gladness and come before Him with joyful singing (Psalm 100:2). Service to God is created for gladness and joy. Unfortunately, my self-driven attempts at working for God have at times created more exhaustion than joyful service.

Shouldn't I be busy all the time for God, serving Him, doing something for Him, being busy, busy, busy?

I talked with a friend who reminded me of God's joy factor, and my response was that I would "work harder" at finding that joy. Seriously? Work harder? Oh dear...

Strength and busyness are not needed by God. God is working, strengthening, energizing, creating the longing and ability to fulfill our purpose for HIS good pleasure! Y'all, that is awesome! You are designed, delivered, saved, and consecrated for a holy calling, a destiny, a life of purpose, through God's purpose and amazing grace!

God, thank You for Your amazing, undeserved favor. Thank You for choosing me and creating me for a divine purpose. Thank You that You will strengthen, energize and create the longing and ability to fulfill my purpose for Your good pleasure.

God's Timeless Truth

Through Jesus we have received "an inheritance [a destiny—we were claimed by God as His own], having been predestined (chosen, appointed beforehand) according to the purpose of Him who works everything in agreement with the counsel and design of His will. ... for He delivered us and saved us and called us with a holy calling [a calling that leads to a consecrated life—a life set apart—a life of purpose], not because of our works [or because of any personal merit—we could do nothing to earn this], but because of His own purpose and grace [His amazing, undeserved favor] which was granted to us in Christ Jesus before the world began [eternal ages ago] (Ephesians 1:11, 2 Timothy 1:9, AMP).

Leaving fingerprints

Standing in my kitchen, a broken item in hand, I applied a quick-drying, super-adhesive to the jagged edges of the glass. The ringing phone drew my attention. Placing the item on the counter, I picked up the receiver. (Yes, this was back when phones were attached the wall).

After my conversation, I hung the phone back in place. Unfortunately, my hand remained firmly attached. Stuck tight, laughing hysterically, and rather embarrassed, I used my convenient mode of communication to call for help. Thanks to a product near and dear to my heart- super-adhesive remover – my hand was freed with no damage.

Weeks later our young son, distraught over a broken toy, found me in the kitchen. Donning my super-mom cape, I grabbed the glue to fix his plastic toy.

He touched my arm. "Are you sure you should do this?"

I patted his hand. "No problem, this is easy."

Eyes-wide, he gulped. "But you're using Super-Glue®."

He did have a point. There had been several incidents with the sticky product I haven't referenced. However, I always fixed what was broken and eventually got unstuck.

I gave him a confident nod. "I'll be careful."

A few squirts in proper places, the broken item reattached, I waited several minutes. His friends gathered around.

Convinced the operation had been a success, I attempted to place the item on the counter. Unfortunately, I was stuck, and I wasn't just stuck, the glue had melted and melded my skin to the plastic. And to top off the problem, I was out of adhesive remover.

After many minutes of begging praying, tugging, pulling, grimacing, and covered in sweat, I handed back the toy. With gasps of appreciation and words like "awesome" and "cool" the boys stared at my handiwork. Thanks to my fingerprints, complete with the top layer of epidermis permanently embedded, my son now held the coolest toy on the block.

My son had my fingerprints on his toy, but what I want to leave with him, and others, are God's fingerprints.

How we live and love, makes an impression. We all have an opportunity to leave the imprint of God. Through God's touch and love, we can touch and love those so needing the touch and love of God.

Heavenly Father, thank You for leaving Your grace-filled imprint on my soul. Help me to touch others with Your love so that they will see the imprint of Your loving touch.

God's Timeless Truth

Whether, then, you eat or drink or whatever you do, do all to the glory of God, and walk in a manner worthy of the God who calls you into His own kingdom and glory (1 Corinthians 10:31, 1 Thessalonians 2:12).

Flame on

I'm at that age. Yes, *that* age. Hot flashes. Argh!
One minute I'm freezing and the next I'm flaming. The heat seems to be worse at night. I'll be nice and snug in my blankets, when all at once my internal regulator switches to super-flame. And when I get hot, the flashes make me hotter.
Why? Why, why, can't they come when I'm freezing?
Sigh... I think I've become a human firefly.
However, the only thing I want burning is my zeal for Christ. I don't want to be cold or lukewarm. I want to flame for God.

I love the story in Luke 24:32 where the men encounter the risen Jesus Christ and afterwards they talked of their hearts burning within them while they spent time with Him.

Encounters with Christ, His word, His truth, and His love, change us. We don't have to be a certain age or gender, (or have hot flashes) to experience a burning heart. Spending time with Jesus, spending time in His Word, kindles the Holy Spirit flame within us.

Even Paul reminded Timothy to kindle afresh, fan into flame, and keep burning for Christ.

The light of Christ burns bright in you, and for you, to shine bright for Him. Flame on!

Heavenly Father, make my heart burn with passion for You, burn for Your word, and Your presence. Let Your light shine in my heart that I may shine brightly for You.
Please keep my flame kindled hot for You!

God's Timeless Truth

"They asked each other, 'Were not our hearts burning within us while he talked with us on the road and opened the Scriptures to us?'" (Luke 24:32)

"For God, who said, 'Light shall shine out of darkness,' is the One who has shone in our hearts to give the Light of the knowledge of the glory of God in the face of Christ" (2 Corinthians 4:6, NASB).

Therefore, "stir up (rekindle the embers of, fan the flame of, and keep burning) the [gracious] gift of God, [the inner fire] that is in you" (2 Timothy 1:6, AMPC).

Alone

Once again, the new person, I sat in my chair in the classroom. Another move, my thirty-sixth move, had brought us to a new city. It's hard to be the new kid, especially when you are no longer a kid. I'm older now, more confident in sitting alone, but there's something about loneliness. Being alone brings attention to itself. Loneliness is really a bully, rather self-focused, always thinking about being alone.

As I sat there trying to not feel alone in my aloneness, I sensed, felt, heard, ... a presence ... from without, yet speaking within, "*I will never leave you.*"

My skin prickled, hair raised on my neck, a quiet joy went deep as I realized I truly was never alone. God is always here. God is always with me. *He is here*. I'm never alone.

You too can be confident, no matter how alone you feel. No matter how lonely you may feel at home, at work, at any location in this vast sea of humanity, you are never alone. God will never leave you or forsake you.

You are never, ever, alone.

God, thank You that you will not, *will not*, ever leave me alone. Thank You that You will never forsake me or leave me. Thank You that You will be with me always to the end of the age and throughout all eternity.

God's Timeless Truth

God promises, I will not fail you. I will never leave you or abandon you. I am with you always. I will not in any way fail you, nor give you up, nor leave you without support. I will not, I will not, I will not in any degree, leave you helpless nor forsake, nor let you down (relax My hold on you)! I will not leave you as orphans [comfortless, desolate, bereaved, forlorn, helpless] .... remember, I am with you always, to the end of the age. (Joshua 1:5, Hebrews 13:5, Matthew 28:20, (Hebrews 13:5, AMPC), (John 14:18, AMPC), (Matthew 28:20, NET).

Rumbling

A teeth-gritting, grinding, metallic rumble signaled a problem with our washer's spin cycle. A repair man was called, who promptly disassembled the washer, showed me the stripped gears, stated the imminent demise of the machine, and pronounced an outrageous fee to fix the problem.

Since, at that time, my husband's job had been outsourced and finances were tight, we politely declined his offer. We prayed for God's favor in keeping the washer working until we were again employed.

Eight months later, my husband continued in his job search and the very noisy washer continued to keep the Buffaloe herd in clean clothing. Then one day, the machine completed the spin cycle without any negative sounds. God fixed the machine!

I shouldn't be surprised; God can do anything. He created the universe and spoke the world into existence. He can definitely fix a washer.

I realize in the grand scheme of things a washer problem is not a major issue, what means so much is that God cares even about the little things in our lives.

Life can be a rumbling mess, spinning with problems and hardships. Please remember that God cares for you. He cares about every little thing and every big thing in your life. God cares for you!

Heavenly Father, thank You that You care about every facet of our lives. Thank You for Your love and provision.

Help me to come to You with my cares, remembering

that Your deep, affectionate love is unfailing and nothing is too difficult for You.

God's Timeless Truth

Jesus said, *'Come to Me and I will give you rest'* (Matthew 11:28).

"Take all your anxieties, all your worries, and all your concerns, once and for all to Him, for He cares about you with deepest affection, and watches over you very carefully" (1 Peter 5:7, AMP).

Will you be one?

Pastor Sonnel, of The Lulu Tree, weeps as he shares the struggles faced by his people in Sierra Leone. Two weeks out of the month, he travels dusty trails to check on people, preaching and seeking out those in need. He then returns home to care for his wife along with the ten orphaned or abandoned children they have taken in their care. He tirelessly shepherds his family and also works at developing businesses to help boys in the villages learn trades.

This one man's example is contagious, and he leaves a trail of shepherds in his wake. Other men have watched Pastor Sonnel and are also stepping up to minister, preach, shepherd, and take in orphans.

One man, one person, can make a difference. Will you be one?

Will you...

Be one in a million like Joshua who stood outside the tent to get as close to God as he could? (Exodus 33:11)

Be like the one leper out of ten who turned back to thank Jesus? (Luke 17:11-19)

Be like the one woman who fell at the feet of Jesus weeping in gratitude? (Luke 7:37-48)

Be like the one man who climbed a tree to see Jesus, and in gratitude, changed his life and followed Jesus? (Luke 19:1-10)

Will you...

Be one in a million like Joshua and Caleb who believed God was big enough to win any battle? (Numbers 13:25-33,

Numbers 14:1-10)

Be as the one who jumped out of the boat to walk on water with Jesus? (Matthew 14:25-29)

Be with those who don't shrink back, but will continue in faith? (Hebrews 10:37-39)

Be with those who have faith to believe and trust God? (Hebrews 11)

Be the one who perseveres through trials and receives the crown of life? (James 1:12)

Be one who will always press on to be with Jesus? (Philippians 3:13-15)

Be one who will run the race to the very end? (Hebrews 12:1, 1 Corinthians 9:24)

Will you be one who runs to God, follows God, thanks God, adores God, serves Him, pressing on to the end, and leaving a trail for others to find God?

Heavenly Father, I'm only one person, but I'm the one You created. Help me to be one who lives for You.

Help me to live in such a way that others will see, and find, the path to You, to be one who always lives fully for You.

God's Timeless Truth

"Therefore, since we have so great a cloud of witnesses surrounding us, let us also lay aside every encumbrance and the sin which so easily entangles us, and let us run with endurance the race that is set before us, fixing our eyes on Jesus..." (Hebrews 12:1-3, NASB).

Keep good records

Day after day, night after night, George Müller made notes of God's faithfulness in his autobiography. I've read and reread Mr. Müller's story many times. His faith and trust in God, along with his meticulous recording of God's faithfulness, encourages me (and many others) to step out in truly believing God will supply all our needs (Philippians 4:19).

Missionaries who have kept diaries and shared letters of the amazing ways God worked, continue to motivate and inspire others to follow in the footsteps of our Savior who tells us to "Go therefore and make disciples of all the nations" (Matthew 28:19).

The stories recorded in the Bible bless us with direction, guidance, encouragement, the road to salvation, and the blessing of knowing better our awesome God.

God keeps beautiful records like the one recorded in Malachi 3:16, "Then those who feared the Lord spoke to one another, and the Lord gave attention and heard it, and a book of remembrance was written before Him for those who fear the Lord and who esteem His name."

Jesus reminds us to "rejoice that your names are recorded in heaven" (Luke 10:20). In God's book, He writes the days ordained for us before we were even born (Psalm 139:16).

God keeps track of our tossing and turning through sleepless nights and each tear is recorded in His ledger (Psalm 56:8, MSG).

God keeps beautiful, meticulous records through His servants to record the things He did for His people.

Let's also be those who keep good records of how God has worked and is working in our lives. Record what God has done in your life and what He is currently doing. Keep a book of remembrance in journals, letters, emails, and in whatever ways you are able to share with others about our wonderful God.

When I first began my writing journey, God highlighted the verse in Habakkuk 2:2, "Then the Lord answered me and said, 'Record the vision and inscribe it on tablets, that the one who reads it may run.'" What I learn through Bible study and time with God, I try to write and share so that others will be drawn to God.

I have a file on my computer and a journal I keep in my Bible for when I'm at church, Bible study, or in my prayer groups. Over the years, I love to look back and see the answers God has given, the ways He has led and guided, and the comfort through hard times. I record my requests and also the answers given by God through His word or His Spirit. Keeping a prayer journal helps us see the power of God at work in our prayer requests. There is such power in reading how God answered in precise ways.

And, when we keep good records, it blesses us and blesses others that will read of the faithfulness of God.

Will you keep good records of what God is doing in your life? Be diligent to document every little thing, every big thing, for all will make a blessed impact for you and others.

Heavenly Father, help me to keep good records of the amazing ways You have worked and continue to work in my life, so that I can look back and be encouraged and also encourage others.

God, please help me to freely share with others all the many ways You are faithful, loving, and kind. Help me to continue to live for You and tell others about You and Your wonderful love.

God's Timeless Truth

"The Lord answered me: 'Write down the vision; write it clearly on clay tablets so whoever reads it can run to tell others'" (Habakkuk 2:2, NCV).

May we be like John who said, "We proclaim to you what we ourselves have actually seen and heard so that you may have fellowship with us. And our fellowship is with the Father and with his Son, Jesus Christ. We are writing these things so that you may fully share our joy" (1 John 1:3-4, NLT).

Great expectations

God has been working on me to fully believe and trust that He is all I need. At times I'll fret and worry before running to God for help. Thankfully, God graciously shows His sufficiency. The process keeps being repeated with various situations. I believe God loves me, I know all things will work to the good, I know He hears when I call, so why do I mentally run around like a chicken with my head cut off instead of trusting Him?

I finally had an "A-ha!" moment when reading a devotion by Mary Southerland on prayer and faith. She related the story of a small country town in need of rain. The pastor of the church called for a prayer meeting to pray and ask God to fill their desperate need. A crowd gathered, and yet the pastor remarked that only one came in faith; he then pointed to a small girl who had brought her umbrella.

Yowza, I forgot my faith umbrella!

There is no difficulty, no problem, and no situation God cannot handle. He provides for every need. God is always faithful. What He begins, He perfects and completes. I need to live in a state of expectation, and bring my faith umbrella, raincoat, and rubber boots!

Heavenly Father, thank You that You hear my prayers. Father, I do believe; help my unbelief. Thank You, God, that nothing is impossible for You.

Help me to live in a state of expectation knowing nothing is too difficult for you. Help me to remember that You do exceedingly, abundantly more than I could ask or imagine.

Thank You that You who began a good work in me will continue until the day of Jesus Christ [right up to the time of His return], developing [that good work] and perfecting and bringing it to full completion (Philippians 1:6, AMP).

Keep working with me, in me, to fully believe with great expectations, for You are a great God!

God's Timeless Truth

Walk by faith, not by sight. Remember nothing is impossible for God (2 Corinthians 5:7, Luke 1:37).

"Trust in the Lord with all your heart and do not lean on your own understanding. In all your ways acknowledge Him, and He will make your paths straight" (Proverbs 3:5-6, NASB).

"'For I know the plans that I have for you', declares the Lord, 'plans for welfare and not for calamity to give you a future and a hope'" (Jeremiah 29:11, NASB).

"Now to Him who is able to do far more abundantly beyond all that we ask or think, according to the power that works within us, to Him be the glory in the church and in Christ Jesus to all generations forever and ever. Amen" (Ephesians 3:20-21, NASB).

Message in a bottle

Day after day, week after week, month after month, and year after year, she wrote a message of love, carefully tucked her note into a bottle and placed it in the ocean.

As the waves carried her message away, she hoped and prayed that one day the bottle would be found and a rescue would take place.

She never stopped writing, never stopped hoping and praying. Even though she wasn't sure what would happen, she knew what was at stake, that lives were lost without the message she had been given to share.

Very few were at her funeral and only a few knew her story. Yet, across the seas in islands and continents far away, her message had been joyfully received. Those who found the bottles, found the truth of a Father' love -- a love that came from heaven, filled with grace, with an offer of eternal life.

The words she shared were words that had brought her hope, joy, and an eternal promise. And so, she wrote the simple message, sharing the story of God's heavenly love.

"For God so loved the world, that He gave His only begotten Son, that whoever believes in Him shall not perish, but have eternal life. For God did not send the Son into the world to judge the world, but that the world might be saved through Him" (John 3:16-17, NASB).

God's joyful message is for you. Will you receive the message?

Will you be faithful to share the message with others?

"Open your hearts to the love God instills... God loves you tenderly. What He gives you is not to be kept under lock and key, but to be shared."
~ Mother Teresa

Dear God, thank You for Your love that sent Your Son to save us. Thank You for Your saving grace. Help me to speak freely and share freely the good news of Your amazing love and wonderful grace.

God's Timeless Truth

Jesus said, "Go, therefore, and make disciples of all nations, baptizing them in the name of the Father and of the Son and of the Holy Spirit, teaching them to observe everything I have commanded you. And remember, I am with you always, to the end of the age" (Matthew 28:19-20, HCSB).

"How beautiful on the mountains are the feet of those who bring good news, who proclaim peace, who bring good tidings, who proclaim salvation, who say to Zion, 'Your God reigns!'" (Isaiah 52:7, NIV).

"My mouth shall tell of Your righteous acts and of Your deeds of salvation all the day, for their number is more than I know." "For we cannot stop speaking about what we have seen and heard" (Acts 4:20, NASB), (Psalm 71:15, AMPC).

Needy

I really wanted something, really, *really* wanted something. I prayed and pursued the thing I desired. The desire even seemed a God-honoring desire. Surely, it was something God would want me to have.

At times, I've whined and been very distracted by my perception of something I thought I needed (or really did need). Eventually, I would give it to God, semi-trusting Him to meet that need. However, I would quickly run back to analyze, stew, and try to fix things in my own power and get that need met in some way or another. Must. Have. Need. Met!

At times, I've needed a friend, needed a spouse, needed a job, needed answers, needed so many things, but what I need to always remember is what Paul shared, "God will liberally supply (fill until full) your every need according to His riches in glory in Christ Jesus." And, God is "able to do exceedingly abundantly above all that we ask or think" (Philippians 4:19, AMP), (Ephesians 3:20, NKJV).

God exceedingly, abundantly supplies for our needs, our *every* need. So, I wondered, was I staring so intently at my need, that God's Kingdom remained hidden?

Stepping away from my need, I asked God to open my eyes to see the blessings He already supplied.

Once my spiritual focus was realigned with God, I realized I had been staring at one thing and missed *every*thing else God was doing in my life.

When I needed a friend, God reminded me of the friends He supplied through family, church, other areas, and especially the ever-present friendship with Him.

When I needed something financially, God showed me how He often provides in unusual ways through coins in the mouth of a fish (Matthew 17:25). He multiplies the little to make much (Matthew 14, Matthew 15), for nothing is ever impossible for Him (Luke 1:37).

All the time, all around you, in **every** need you have, God is pouring out His blessings. God works in **every** thing. Remember, God's exceeding, abundant provision is more than we could ask or imagine. God's love is with you through every lovely and every unlovely moment. God's grace and mercy are there for every need of grace and mercy. God's healing is available for every wound. God's blessings endure forever, His love and friendship never fail, He is with you always.

Do you have a need? Ask God to show you how He is working. Ask Him to show you how to refocus your focus on His Kingdom perspective.

Heavenly Father, You promise to provide for all my needs, therefore, help me to see Your Kingdom perspective by refocusing my focus on You. Help me to see what You have already provided.

Help me not to be anxious about tomorrow, because You are already there in my every tomorrow. Help me to know the difference between my wants and my needs. Enlarge my vision and my understanding to see how You are working.

Help me to remember nothing is impossible for You and Your grace is sufficient for all my needs. Help me to not miss how You are working in every day of my life. Thank You, Father!

God's Timeless Truth

"The Lord is my shepherd; I have everything I need" (Psalm 23:1, NCV).

"The Lord listens to those in need and does not look down on captives" (Psalm 69:33, NCV).

"For He delivers the needy when he calls out, the poor also and him who has no helper. He will have pity on the poor and weak and needy and will save the lives of the needy" (Psalm 72:12-13, AMPC).

"He will have compassion on the poor and needy, and the lives of the needy he will save" (Psalm 72:13, NASB).

"And we know [with great confidence] that God [who is deeply concerned about us] causes all things to work together [as a plan] for good for those who love God, to those who are called according to His plan and purpose" (Romans 8:28, AMP). "Do not worry about anything, but pray and ask God for everything you need, always giving thanks. And God's peace, which is so great we cannot understand it, will keep your hearts and minds in Christ Jesus" (Philippians 4:6-7, NCV).

Overwhelmed

"Please listen and answer me, for I am overwhelmed by my troubles. From the ends of the earth, I cry to you for help when my heart is overwhelmed. Lead me to the towering rock of safety, for you are my safe refuge, a fortress where my enemies cannot reach me" (Psalm 61:2-3, Psalm 55:2, NLT).

Heart pounding, I gripped the kitchen counter. Anxiety and stress had overtaken, and I couldn't get myself under control. Day and night my mind raced as desperate prayers begged heaven for a loved one. I couldn't find rest, nor find the balance between praying like crazy and not going crazy. Prayer needs were overwhelming, life was overwhelming, everything seemed overwhelming. Ack! I needed to get over the whelming!

I knew God was once again attempting to teach me to trust Him more, to believe His power and goodness, and to believe what He had shared years earlier in a time of prayer for my loved one. I believed, but my unbelief had robbed me of my joy and rest.

While attending a Big Daddy Weave concert, one of the men shared "*What overwhelms you, owns you.*"

Ouch!

That sure put things into perspective.

I don't want to be overwhelmed by anything, or anyone, other than Jesus.

I need to put my perspective back where it belongs, the place where freedom, answers, peace, guidance, wisdom, and eternal love are found.

I need to remember who God is and remember the truths He gives us in His Word.

To break overwhelming thoughts, remember...God made a way for the Israelites to cross over the Red Sea by parting the waters and destroying their pursuing enemies (Exodus 14:13-30). God helped the Israelites cross over the flood-stage Jordan River to the promised land (Joshua 3).

God helped His people step over the ruins of the walls of Jericho to be victorious against their enemies (Joshua 6).

God's power is big enough to help us cross over any concern or problem, He will part the way before us and help us step over and through the ruins to victory against any enemy.

When anxious thoughts multiply and overwhelm, when footing is slipping, God and His word bring comfort... "When I said, my foot is slipping, Your mercy and loving-kindness, O Lord, held me up. In the multitude of my [anxious] thoughts within me, Your comforts cheer and delight my soul!" (Psalm 94:18-19, AMPC).

When peace can't be found, Isaiah returns focus... "You will keep in perfect and constant peace the one whose mind is steadfast [that is, committed and focused on You—in both inclination and character], because he trusts and takes refuge in You [with hope and confident expectation]. Trust [confidently] in the Lord forever [He is your fortress, your shield, your banner], for the Lord God is an everlasting Rock [the Rock of Ages]" (Isaiah 26:3-4, AMP).

When the way is unknown, God's Word reminds... "You will make known to me the path of life; in Your presence is fullness of joy; in Your right hand there are pleasures forever" (Psalm 16:11, NASB).

When burdens are so heavy, Jesus beckons... "Come to Me, all who are weary and heavy-laden, and I will give you rest. Take My yoke upon you and learn from Me, for I am gentle and humble in heart, and you will find rest for your souls" (Matthew 11:28-29, NASB).

When the sorrow of past sins torment and overwhelm, "My guilt has overwhelmed me like a burden too heavy to bear. Though we are overwhelmed by our sins, you forgive them all. In Christ we are set free by the blood of his death, and so we have forgiveness of sins. How rich is God's grace" (Psalm 65:3, NLT; Psalm 38:4, NIV; Ephesians 1:7, NCV).

Jesus reminds again where peace is found... "I have told you these things, so that in Me you may have [perfect] peace and confidence. In the world you have tribulation and trials and distress and frustration; but be of good cheer [take courage; be confident, certain, undaunted]! For I have overcome the world. [I have deprived it of power to harm you and have conquered it for you]" (John 16:33, AMPC).

Even when burdens are heavy, even when life is overwhelming, God's Truth holds firm. "Can anything ever separate us from Christ's love? Does it mean He no longer loves us if we have trouble or calamity, or are persecuted, or hungry, or destitute, or in danger, or threatened with death? ... No, despite all these things, overwhelming victory is ours through Christ, who loved us. And I am convinced that nothing can ever separate us from God's love. Neither death nor life, neither angels nor demons, neither our fears for today nor our worries about tomorrow—not even the powers of hell can separate us from God's love" (Romans 8:35-38, NLT).

Paul blesses with another reminder... "Do not fret or

have any anxiety about anything, but in every circumstance and in everything, by prayer and petition (definite requests), with thanksgiving, continue to make your wants known to God. And God's peace [shall be yours, that tranquil state of a soul assured of its salvation through Christ, and so fearing nothing from God and being content with its earthly lot of whatever sort that is, that peace] which transcends all understanding shall garrison and mount guard over your hearts and minds in Christ Jesus" (Philippians 4:6-7, AMPC).

In these overwhelming times, turn the focus off the problems and back on our Savior. Be like those who "When the crowd saw Jesus, they were overwhelmed with awe, and they ran to greet Him" (Mark 9:15, NLT).

Overwhelmed with awe by the love of our Savior, Jesus Christ, we find confident, undaunted courage, and peace in His loving, overcoming, conquering power.

Relieved, happy sigh...

Heavenly Father, so often life is hard, difficult, messy, and overwhelming. Thank You that nothing is impossible for You. Thank You that nothing can separate us from Your love. Please help me look up to You, to see You, trust You, and give all my worries to You. I want to be only overwhelmed with awe by You and Your great love.

God's Timeless Truth

Please take time to read again the Bible verses.

The great heist

Two men hatched a plot and bought the abandoned building on Main Street. They didn't talk to anyone, just went to the building in the morning and left late at night. Across the street, old-timers on the front porch of the General Store, watched and wondered what the two strangers were doing day-after-day in secret.

One night when the stores were closed, a boom shook the small town. People ran to see what happened. Dust and debris filled the air and a huge crater now stood next to the bank.

Screams and desperate yells came from the pit. The two strangers, covered in sewage, tried to claw their way out of the nasty, slimy hole they had created. The men thought they had tunneled to the bank and dynamited the vault, but instead blasted open a concrete sewage tank.

One of my older relatives chuckled as he told the story from years ago in his small town. Crime definitely didn't pay in this instance.

Sin also doesn't pay. The devil makes many promises, even makes sin look like a sure-fire way to get what is wanted. But, just like these unfortunate criminals, sin only leaves a slimy mess. "Evil people fall into their own traps; good people run the other way, glad to escape" (Proverbs 29:6, MSG).

Fortunately, the grace of God reaches down to rescue those trapped in their pits of sin.

For those who call to His Son, Jesus Christ for help, His merciful love washes away the repentant sinner's stains and leaves them white as snow.

"Because of love, there is no depth to which you can go that the grace of God will not go further still. There is no extent to which sin can get a hold of your life that the immensity of His salvation will not extend beyond the sin to keep it from overtaking you. There is no sin in your life that is causing you to stumble for which God has not more than adequately provided a solution."
~ Henry & Richard Blackaby[i]

God, thank You no matter how messy my sin, how deep in the pit of sin I may be, Your strong arm is never too short to save and Your mercies are new every morning. Thank You for Your loving grace that washes away my sin, cleanses, and gives me a new life in You. Help me to remember that no one is beyond Your grace. Thank You, Father.

God's Timeless Truth

Take hope and take heart, "For God so loved the world that He gave His only begotten Son, that whoever believes in Him should not perish but have everlasting life.

For God did not send His Son into the world to condemn the world, but that the world through Him might be saved" (John 3:16-17, NKJV).

Rejoice that "In Him we have redemption through His blood, the forgiveness of sins, according to the riches of His grace. For we do not have a High Priest who cannot sympathize with our weaknesses, but was in all points tempted as we are, yet without sin. Let us therefore come boldly to the throne of grace, that we may obtain mercy and find grace to help in time of need" (Ephesians 1:7 NKJV, Hebrews 4:15-16, NKJV).

Therefore, "Come now, and let us reason together," says the Lord, "Though your sins are like scarlet, they shall be as white as snow; though they are red like crimson, they shall be as wool" (Isaiah 1:18, NKJV).

Don't camp there

Stuck?

With all the horrible, nasty stuff that comes our way, it's very easy to get stuck in the pain, stuck in lost dreams, stuck in the loss, stuck in the terrible thing that happened.

Making breakfast one morning, a memory of a very difficult time replayed in my thoughts. Blindsided, I reeled as the horrifying scene replayed. For a few minutes, I pondered what to do -- seek more counseling, mull it over again in my head, withdraw from the world, or move on. I had a choice, I could grieve, get angry, or move on.

What happened, all the bad things over the years can't be changed. However, I have a choice on stopping at the places of heartache and tragedy or move forward. I can't change what happened, I can't fix what was done to me by others, but I don't have to stay in those memories. I can give them to God.

What happened in the past, whether it was something done to us or something we have done, we can't change, but with God comes amazing changes.

In Exodus 14, the Israelites were trapped at the Red Sea complaining to Moses about what seems like their demise by the hands of the pursuing Egyptians. Moses told the people to stand still and God would fight for them. However, God responded and asked Moses, "Why are you crying out to Me? Tell the sons of Israel to go forward."

Other Bible versions have "move forward," "break camp," "get moving!"

When the Israelites were camped at the Red Sea, they couldn't see any way to move forward.

What looked like a completely impossible situation with no hope for rescue, no hope for a future, God turned into a miraculous lifesaving, life-changing event.

To move forward to something new, you have to exit the old. Beyond your Red Sea difficulties, lay the promised land. Let God lead you to the other side.

No matter what has happened in your life, what problems you faced, or whatever you face at present, you don't have to stay camped at that spot. Move forward with God. He will lead in the way you should go -- the lifesaving, life-changing way.

Break camp. On the other side of your broken places, the mountain of problems, trust God to lead you to the other side.

Break camp, new life is waiting. God is always doing new things, opening new doors, bringing new healing, and new restoration.

Don't camp on your achievements, or lack of achievements, move forward into the new day God has for you. Jesus calls, beckons for you to break camp and release your burdens to Him, "Come to Me, all you who labor and are heavy-laden and overburdened, and I will cause you to rest. I will ease and relieve and refresh your souls" (Matthew 11:28, AMPC).

God is a miracle working God, nothing is too hard for Him. Nothing is impossible for God.

Break camp and move forward through the power, mercy, grace, healing, redemption, and restoration of our amazing Savior, Jesus Christ.

Don't give up. Don't give up. Don't give up! Move on!

Jesus, I come to You. I need rest from these burdens. Thank You that nothing is too hard for You. Thank You that You work miracles and ***nothing*** is impossible for You. Help me to move on. I want to see the new thing that You are doing. Lead me and guide me out of the wilderness with Your saving grace, mercy, and love.

God's Timeless Truth

"...the Lord our God said to us, 'You have stayed at this mountain long enough. It is time to break camp and move on. Go..." (Deuteronomy 1:6-7, NLT).

"I will lead the blind by a way they do not know, in paths they do not know I will guide them. I will make darkness into light before them and rugged places into plains. These are the things I will do, and I will not leave them undone" (Isaiah 42:16, NASB).

"Forget the former things; do not dwell on the past. See, I am doing a new thing! Now it springs up; do you not perceive it? I am making a way in the wilderness and streams in the wasteland" (Isaiah 43:18-19, NIV). Remember to "...focus on this one thing: Forgetting the past and looking forward to what lies ahead" (Philippians 3:13, NLT).

Specific set of skills

The devil messed with my family and I was angry! I do not take vengeance on people because I trust God's vengeance. However, I will fight back. I have been given a very specific set of skills, and I will use them to make the enemy pay by telling as many people as possible about our healing, restoring, forgiving, merciful, loving God.

I don't have the answers, but God does. I can't solve the world's problems, but God can. I don't have the resources to provide for everyone's needs, but I can share the Good News given by God. I write to share the Good News of Jesus Christ. Every book I've written is to help others be drawn to God's hope, joy, peace, encouragement, comfort, and restoration through our healing, loving God.

You too have been given a very specific set of skills to share God's Good News. No one else has your story, no one else has walked your journey, and no one else can share as you can share.

You are needed. You are gifted to help others, gifted to work and bless, and share the love of Christ.

"Christ gave gifts to people—he made some to be apostles, some to be prophets, some to go and tell the Good News, and some to have the work of caring for and teaching God's people. Christ gave those gifts to prepare God's holy people for the work of serving, to make the body of Christ stronger" (Ephesians 4:11-12, NCV).

You are gifted. Yes, you! You are gifted with extraordinary power, divine grace through the Holy Spirit. You are gifted to display, exhibit, and give clear evidence of our marvelous God.

We are all given distinct gifts and areas where we are called to minister. God is the one who gifts and gives what is needed. "For it is God who is at work in you, both to will and to work for His good pleasure" (Philippians 2:13 NASB). You were created for pleasure to enjoy the pleasure of God's company. And in that pleasure of God working within you, He gifts You with skill.

Therefore, please tell others about God in whatever way God has blessed you to share. Use your specific set of skills for His glory!

Heavenly Father, thank You that You have equipped me and given me a specific set of skills. Please open my eyes to see the skills You have given and help me to use them for Your glory.

God's Timeless Truth

"there are distinctive varieties and distributions of endowments (gifts, extraordinary powers distinguishing certain Christians, due to the power of divine grace operating in their souls by the Holy Spirit) and they vary, but the [Holy] Spirit remains the same. And there are distinctive varieties of service and ministration, but it is the same Lord [Who is served]. And there are distinctive varieties of operation [of working to accomplish things], but it is the same God Who inspires and energizes them all in all. But to each one is given the manifestation of the [Holy] Spirit [the evidence, the spiritual illumination of the Spirit] for good and profit" (1 Corinthians 12:4-7, AMPC).

Not consumed

Desperate for a breakthrough, for change and help, my prayers pounded on heaven's door for loved ones, for those hurting, ill, weak and frail, for those suffering loss, grief and pain, and for those who have wandered away from God.

Despair threatened to consume, and then I remembered God's promises. Because of God's never-failing compassions and loving-kindness, we are not consumed. His unfailing love provides abundant stability and faithfulness, new every morning for every need. (Lamentations 3:21-24).

God, who kept the burning bush from being consumed (Exodus 3:1-2), will also keep you from being consumed. The same God who kept Shadrach, Meshach, and Abednego safe in the fire, will also be with you in the fires of life (Daniel 3).

Our God is a consuming fire (Hebrews 12:29), consuming the sin from our lives through the forgiveness and grace of His Son, Jesus Christ.

When trials and difficulties attack family and friends, remember God's mercies and compassion will also be available for our family and friends. Our hope, their hope, will not be consumed.

God promises, "when you pass through the waters, I will be with you; and when you pass through the rivers, they will not sweep over you. When you walk through the fire, you will not be burned; the flames will not set you ablaze. For I am the Lord your God, the Holy One of Israel, your Savior" (Isaiah 43:2-3a, NIV).

Hold on to the hope that will never let go, for God's compassion, mercy, and faithfulness will never fail.

Thank You Father for Your all-consuming, never-ending mercy, compassion, and love. Consume me in Your love. Thank You that as Your child nothing can consume me, for I am eternally safe with You.

God's Timeless Truth

I recall and have hope and expectation. Because of the Lord's mercies and loving-kindness, we are not consumed. His tender compassions never fail. They are new every morning; great is His abundant stability and faithfulness. 'The Lord is my portion,' says my soul, therefore I hope in Him!' (Lamentations 3:21-24).

Keep updating

If I don't keep my website software up to date, my site is prone to attacks. And, my little website stays under attack -- almost 5000 hits one day from hackers and bots around the world as they tried to gain access. My security software programs run constantly, and I make sure they keep running and updated at all times.

In the same way, we need to make sure our minds are updated with God's word. If we don't continue reading and studying God's Word, we are prone to more attacks of the enemy to twist and manipulate God's truth.

Without the truth from the Bible, we are more prone to false teaching, depression, and negative issues with our bodies and minds.

Reading God's word helps us to obey and be blessed by His word. Jesus said, "blessed are those who hear the word of God and observe it" (Luke 11:28).

The Bible is our offensive weapon which is the sword of the Spirit (Ephesians 6:17). The Bible blesses us with a weapon to fight against Satan and the lies of this world.

Even though I have been a Christian for decades, I still see new truths and exciting new discoveries as I read and reread passages.

The more we read the Bible, the more truth is found, and the deeper truth is ingrained in our spirits and thoughts.

The Bible keeps our souls fed and nourished, enriched with the life-giving Truth. God's living water keeping us spiritually hydrated. Treasure sought in God's word, brings forth rich treasure.

As we read and study, the Holy Spirit illuminates and

opens our mind to understand things hidden from the foundation of the world.

The Bible is alive, powerful, active, energizing, and equipping. Through Bible study we are trained, corrected, instructed, renewed, and restored. For your protection, keep your mind safe, secure, and updated in God's word.

"A Bible that's falling apart usually belongs to someone who isn't." ~ Charles Spurgeon

Heavenly Father, help me to spend time in the Bible, Your word. Thank You that Your Word is alive, active, and full of power, and is given by divine inspiration to help me learn and grow.

Thank You as I read the Bible, I'm given instruction to know when I've sinned and how I can receive forgiveness. Thank You that the Bible helps me be equipped for every day that I live. Thank You that Your word trains and teaches me how to live in a way that pleases You.

God's Timeless Truth

Jesus said, "It is written, 'Man is not to live on bread only. Man is to live by every word that God speaks'" (Matthew 4:4, NLV).

"For the Word that God speaks is alive and full of power [making it active, operative, energizing, and effective]; it is sharper than any two-edged sword, penetrating to the dividing line of the breath of life (soul) and [the immortal] spirit, and of joints and marrow [of the deepest parts of our nature], exposing and sifting and analyzing and judging the very thoughts and purposes of the heart" (Hebrews 4:12, AMPC).

"All Scripture is God-breathed [given by divine inspiration] and is profitable for instruction, for conviction [of sin], for correction [of error and restoration to obedience], for training in righteousness [learning to live in conformity to God's will, both publicly and privately—behaving honorably with personal integrity and moral courage]; so that the man of God may be complete and proficient, outfitted and thoroughly equipped for every good work" (2 Timothy 3:16-17, AMP).

"Don't copy the behavior and customs of this world, but let God transform you into a new person by changing the way you think. Then you will learn to know God's will for you, which is good and pleasing and perfect" (Romans 12:2, NLT).

"Study and do your best to present yourself to God approved, a workman [tested by trial] who has no reason to be ashamed, accurately handling and skillfully teaching the word of truth" (2 Timothy 2:15, AMP).

Rats with good PR

My sweet husband is not a fan of squirrels. He doesn't like that they steal the bird food from our feathered friends. He calls squirrels rats with good public relations.

I, on the other hand, think squirrels are cute. I think of them as squirrel pups or squirrel kittens. I love their little fluffy tails and that they can accomplish mighty feats of acrobatics to access food from bird feeders.

I even thought about buying a squirrel feeder, but then, I read that some squirrels aren't always vegetarians -- when hungry they can turn carnivorous. Okay, that kinda makes me uncomfortable. Squirrels don't seem quite so cute now. Their public relations have taken a hit.

Makes me remember that Satan often tries to disguise sin in a positive manner. The devil tries to convince the world that sin isn't "that" wrong and they are just sweet little fluffy things.

Sin is never a sweet, little fluffy thing. No matter how "good" the public relations are about sin, sin is a big rat, a carnivorous monster, eating the sinner from the inside out.

There is nothing pretty about sin. Sin is **never** your friend.

Don't believe the lies from the enemy, don't even believe your eyes and emotions. Sin is never you friend.

Please don't coddle sin, don't let it in your yard, in your home, in your mind, and in your life.

Sin's temptations will come, but Jesus is always ready to save, always with enough power to help you through.

God, help me remember sin is never good. Thank You

that although we all are tempted, You always have given us the ability to run from temptation. Thank You that You will give us the power to resist and always give us a way to escape. Please help me get rid of any sin in my life that keeps me from You. Help me to honor You in my life because of the precious gift of Your forgiveness and mercy.

God's Timeless Truth

When temptations come, "be subject to God. Resist the devil [stand firm against him], and he will flee from you" (James 4:7, AMPC).

"The temptations in your life are no different from what others experience. And God is faithful. He will not allow the temptation to be more than you can stand. When you are tempted, he will show you a way out so that you can endure" (1 Corinthians 10:13, NLT).

"So, do not let sin control your life here on earth so that you do what your sinful self wants to do" (Romans 6:12, NCV).

"Shun immorality and all sexual looseness [flee from impurity in thought, word, or deed]. Any other sin which a man commits is one outside the body, but he who commits sexual immorality sins against his own body. Do you not know that your body is the temple (the very sanctuary) of the Holy Spirit Who lives within you, whom you have received [as a Gift] from God? You are not your own, you were bought with a price [purchased with a preciousness and paid for, made His own]. So then, honor God and bring glory to Him in your body" (1 Corinthians 6:18-20, AMPC).

Dwelling in life

One night I dreamed my sweet husband and I were driving in the mountains. When we turned a corner, people were in the middle of the street where they had fallen on ice and snow. Slipping and sliding, the people could not find their footing.

The dream reminds me of what is happening in our world. People are slipping and sliding, stumbling, and falling, because they are not standing firm on (and in) the word of God. A secure footing can't be found without God's word, and God's guidance can't be received without knowing The Word – Jesus Christ.

Throughout the Bible, this statement is made, "The word of the Lord came to..." God's word came to people to guide, warn, and bring encouragement and hope.

God continues speaking, yet I wonder how many will listen. Would we know the word of the Lord if it came to us? Reading the word of the Lord, the Bible, helps us to hear and know The Word.

Jesus, the Word, became flesh and dwelt among us. For those who invite Him into their lives, He dwells within them. As we dwell in the life given through Jesus Christ, we become united in His Spirit. Jesus said His sheep hear His voice, they know Him, and they follow Him (John 10:27).

How cool is that? Jesus, The Word, dwells in us and His Holy Spirit brings guidance, comfort, and encouragement. Jesus is the Life, and with a relationship with Him we dwell in His life.

As we read God's word, we are reading The Word, and are given insight and wisdom not found in this world.

God's word is filled with power, active and alive, bringing living water renewal to thirsty souls. Stand firm in these slippery times by reading the Bible. God's word brings you healing, hope, joy, wisdom, encouragement, perfect peace, setting free and bringing light to guide your feet and a lamp for your path.

Renew your mind with scripture, fill your thoughts with God's word, study and meditate on the verses. God's word is an indispensable weapon in the fight against demonic forces and the lies of the enemy.

Every time you read God's word; the truth will dwell deeper in your life as you dwell deeper in the One who brings life.

Heavenly Father, thank You for Your Word. Thank You for Jesus and thank You for the Bible. Thank You that when I give my life to Jesus, I am blessed to dwell in His eternal life.

Father, help me to meditate on Your word throughout the day and night. Your promise is that I will be blessed, happy, fortunate, soul-prosperous, and enviable when I delight in and desire Your precepts, instructions, and teachings. As I meditate on Your Word and observe what You have written, You will help me deal wisely and have good success.

Help me ponder and study Your word, because then I will be like a tree firmly planted and tended by the streams of water, ready to bring forth its fruit in its season; its leaf also shall not fade or wither; and everything he does shall prosper and come to maturity.

God's Timeless Truth

"This Book of the Law shall not depart out of your mouth, but you shall meditate on it day and night, that you may observe and do according to all that is written in it. For then you shall make your way prosperous, and then you shall deal wisely and have good success" (Joshua 1:8, AMPC).

"For the Word that God speaks is alive and full of power [making it active, operative, energizing, and effective]; it is sharper than any two-edged sword, penetrating to the dividing line of the breath of life (soul) and [the immortal] spirit, and of joints and marrow [of the deepest parts of our nature], exposing and sifting and analyzing and judging the very thoughts and purposes of the heart" (Hebrews 4:12, AMPC).

"Every Scripture is God-breathed (given by His inspiration) and profitable for instruction, for reproof and conviction of sin, for correction of error and discipline in obedience, [and] for training in righteousness (in holy living, in conformity to God's will in thought, purpose, and action), so that the man of God may be complete and proficient, well fitted and thoroughly equipped for every good work" (2 Timothy 3:16-17, AMPC).

"Oh, the joys of those who do not follow the advice of the wicked, or stand around with sinners, or join in with mockers. But they delight in the law of the Lord, meditating on it day and night. They are like trees planted along the riverbank, bearing fruit each season. Their leaves never wither, and they prosper in all they do" (Psalm 1:1-3, NLT).

Crossing to joy

The cross and laying down our lives to carry our cross to follow Jesus Christ, do not seem like positive topics that bring joy. However, the cross of Jesus Christ shows the depth of our sins and the depth of our Father's love. For God so loved the world that He gave His Son in our place for our sins.

Without the cross, without the sacrifice Jesus made for our sins, without His resurrection, without His conquering sin and death, making payment for our sins, there is no saving grace, no good works good enough without the cross of Jesus. The cross is the bridge, the way to cross-over to eternal life.

Without the cross there wouldn't have been a resurrection. Crucifixion was the worst way to die, yet because of the sacrifice of Jesus Christ on the cross, we are offered God's best, grace-filled freedom.

The power of Christ resurrects anything and anyone, for nothing is impossible for God. The power of Christ's resurrection revives our lost lives, our lost hope, and our lost joy.

Carrying our cross isn't a burden, it is the symbol of freedom. The cross we carry shows we identify with the cross of Christ where Jesus took all our sins and nailed them to His cross so that we could be free and have access to our loving Heavenly Father.

Carrying our cross symbolizes we have laid down our life to follow and serve the One who went to the cross, died, and rose again to give us eternal life.

Jesus said, "Take up your cross and follow Me" (Luke

9:23). Taking up your cross to follow Jesus is an invitation to lay down your life to pick up His resurrected, eternal life. Because of the cross, your sins are forgiven. Because of Jesus Christ's death on the cross, those who believe in Him, turn to Him, give their lives to Him, are delivered from the power of sin and death (Romans 8:2). Happy, blessed, and fortunate is the one whose sins have been forgiven (Psalm 32:1-2).

Pick up your cross and follow is not an invitation for a life of drudgery, it is an invitation to new, never-ending, amazing joy-filled life through the power, might, glory, peace, hope, encouragement, courage, comfort, compassion, kindness, and unfailing love of Jesus Christ.

Love held Jesus on the cross. Love resurrected Jesus from the grave. Love offers forgiveness, hope, and eternal life. Because of the cross, your life is given mercy and grace and joyfully resurrected.

> *"Jesus died on the cross for you, and the Scripture says that you can never be the same once you have been to the Cross: 'If anyone is in Christ, he is a new creation; old things have passed away; behold, all things have become new (2 Corinthians 5:17, NKJV).'"*
> *~ Billy Graham*

Cross to eternal joy by following The One who went to the cross for you.

Jesus, thank You for Your sacrifice. Thank You for going to the cross for my sins. Thank You that because You went to the cross, I am free to accept Your grace and mercy so that I can cross to eternal joy with You!

> *"We owe all to Jesus crucified. What is your life, my brethren, but the cross? Whence comes the bread of your soul but from the cross? What is your joy but the cross? What is your delight, what is your heaven, but the Blessed One, once crucified for you, whoever lives to make intercession for you?"*
> *~ Charles H. Spurgeon[ii]*

God's Timeless Truth

"Our old way of life was nailed to the cross with Christ, a decisive end to that sin-miserable life—no longer at sin's every beck and call! What we believe is this: If we get included in Christ's sin-conquering death, we also get included in his life-saving resurrection. We know that when Jesus was raised from the dead it was a signal of the end of death-as-the-end. Never again will death have the last word. When Jesus died, he took sin down with him, but alive he brings God down to us. From now on, think of it this way: Sin speaks a dead language that means nothing to you; God speaks your mother tongue, and you hang on every word. You are dead to sin and alive to God. That's what Jesus did" (Romans 6:6-11, MSG).

Drowning

Do you feel as though you are drowning? Would you join me in prayer?
    Lord. I can't hold on. Please save me. Please save my loved ones. Please, Lord. I'm drowning. Please save me and save them! The waves of problems are like a tidal wave on my soul. I can't take another hurt, heartache, or tragedy. I'm drowning, Lord. Please save.
    Show me how to live and how to love in the midst of a world that destroys life and doesn't love. Show me how to stand when I'm too weak to stand. Show me how to fight against evil and not be overcome by evil. Show me how to love with your love before my love grows cold from the heat of the battles.
    My distressed prayers pound on heaven's door, my soul cries out for You to save those I love and rescue those who need You. Please rescue them. Comfort those who mourn and grieve, heal those who are sick, open eyes blinded by sin, open hearts that have grown hard, reveal Yourself, Lord. Reveal Yourself to those who have wandered away from You. Reveal Your love. Destroy the lies of Satan. Restore, redeem, and create good from what the enemy meant for evil.
    The storms hit hard; the waves break over my soul. Lord, save. I'm going to drown! I am sick at heart. How long, O Lord, until you restore me?
    Return, O Lord, and rescue me. Save me because of your unfailing love. I come to you for protection, O Lord my God. Save me—rescue me!
    Show me Your unfailing love in wonderful ways. By

your mighty power You rescue those who seek refuge from their enemies.

The reminder comes of Jesus' disciples trapped in the storm, fearful and afraid. Jesus responded, "Why are you afraid? You have so little faith!" Then He got up and rebuked the wind and waves, and suddenly there was a great calm (Matthew 8:26). Jesus, thank You that no storm is too big for You. Calm my soul, Lord.

God's truth rushes to rescue, and grants grace that breathes into my drowning soul. His love casts out my fear. His truth reminds me to be still, to not be afraid for He is with me. To not be discouraged, for He is my God. He will strengthen and help me. He will hold me up with His victorious right hand.

Heavenly Father, thank You for Your peace. Thank You that You will strengthen and hold me up. Your lovingkindness calms me as I rest in Your love. I will not be afraid for You, God, are with me. Thank You for rescuing and catching me in Your strong arms. Thank You for Your protection and comfort, Father.

Thank You that You love those I love even more than I can imagine. Thank You that Your strong arm is mighty to save. Thank You that nothing is impossible for You and nothing is too hard for You.

Thank You, Heavenly Father. Thank You.

God's Timeless Truth

God caught me "reached all the way from sky to sea; he pulled me out of that ocean of hate, that enemy chaos, the void in which I was drowning. They hit me when I was down, but God stuck by me. He stood me up on a wide-open field; I stood there saved—surprised to be loved! For the Lord your God is living among you. He is a mighty savior. He will take delight in you with gladness. With his love, he will calm all your fears. He will rejoice over you with joyful songs."

"The Lord is my shepherd; I have all that I need. He lets me rest in green meadows; He leads me beside peaceful streams. He renews my strength. He guides me along right paths, bringing honor to His name."

"Even when I walk through the darkest valley, I will not be afraid, for You are close beside me. Your rod and your staff protect and comfort me. You prepare a feast for me in the presence of my enemies. You honor me by anointing my head with oil. My cup overflows with blessings. Surely your goodness and unfailing love will pursue me all the days of my life, and I will live in the house of the Lord forever." (Matthew 8:25, Psalm 6:3-4, Psalm 7:1, Psalm 17:7, 1 John 4:18, Matthew 8:24-26, Mark 4:39, Isaiah 41:10, Psalm 46:10-11, Matthew 19:26, Jeremiah 32:27, Psalm 18:16-19, MSG; Zephaniah 3:17, NLT; Psalm 23, NLT)

What if you knew?

What if you knew how **much** you are loved? What if you really, really, **really believed** God loved you?

Would you see God, yourself, your life, and others differently?

Would you believe that, know that, live that, remember that all things work for the good because your Heavenly Father loves you; really, really, really loves you?

What if you knew how much you are loved? Would you stop beating yourself up for your mistakes? Would you forgive yourself and others so that you can live free in the forgiveness of God, trusting Him to make you right, to make all things right?

What if you knew how much you are loved? Would you give God your regrets, your sins, your wayward ways, remembering God is the Father waiting with love for the prodigal to return home? Would you remember that nothing can separate you from God's love?

What if you knew how much you are loved? Would you stop looking back and instead look up, would you trust that God loves you enough, loves you so much, that His love covers your past, present, and future? Would you move forward with excitement because you know you are loved?

What if you knew how much you are loved? Would you remember God is the Father who sent His son to earth for your rescue?

Would you remember Jesus came willingly for you, to save you, to free you, to give you an eternal, hope-filled, joyful home? Would you, could you, will you, relax and rest in God's love?

What if you lived believing you are truly loved by God? God's love is unfailing and everlasting because God's love is not just an emotion, **God *is* love**. What if you let God's love wash over you, filling you, restoring you, mending you, cleansing you, setting you forever free?

What if you knew, really knew, how much you were loved?

Oh Father, I believe, help my unbelief. Help me to know You, for You are love. Let me swim, diving deep into the beauty of Your everlasting kindness and unfailing love. Help me to know, and always remember, how much I am loved by You.

God's Timeless Truth

Remember, the love of God sent His loving Son to lovingly save you. "God so loved the world that He gave His only begotten Son, that whoever believes in Him should not perish but have everlasting life. For God did not send His Son into the world to condemn the world, but that the world through Him might be saved" (John 3:16-17, NKJV).

God loves with an everlasting love (Jeremiah 31:3). God is good; His lovingkindness is everlasting and His faithfulness is to all generations (Psalm 100:5).

We can't even imagine what God has planned for those who love Him. "Eye has not seen, nor ear heard, nor have entered into the heart of man the things which God has prepared for those who love Him" (1 Corinthians 2:9, NKJV).

Be convinced "that neither death, nor life, nor angels, nor principalities, nor things present, nor things to come, nor powers, nor height, nor depth, nor any other created thing, will be able to separate us from the love of God, which is in Christ Jesus our Lord" (Romans 8:38-39, NASB).

"I have loved you just as the Father has loved Me; remain in My love [and do not doubt My love for you]" (John 15:9, AMP).

For, "whoever confesses that Jesus is the Son of God, God abides in him, and he in God. We have come to know and have believed the love which God has for us. God is love, and the one who abides in love abides in God, and God abides in him. By this, love is perfected with us, so that we may have confidence in the day of judgment..." (1 John 4:15-17, NASB).

The shining ones

Looking for a way to cope, tears flowed as I banged my fists against the wall. The devil had again attacked my family and left pieces of my heart scattered on the ground.

You too have been wounded. Satan is out to destroy, leaving behind scars and nightmarish memories. I'm so sorry for what you have been through. I'm so sorry for the pain you have experienced -- the pain that ripped open your heart.

And now, the devil lies to you that your broken places will bleed brokenness, that you won't ever heal, and your life will never be the same. The devil lies because of what happened, you have no hope of your dream coming to fruition, and because of what happened, you can't be the person you wanted to be. The devil is a liar!

May I share hope with you?

Kintsugi is the Japanese art of repairing broken pottery with lacquer dusted or mixed with powdered gold, silver, or platinum. What was broken is repaired with precious metal. What was broken becomes a work of art. What was shattered now glows with beauty.

Are you broken?

When you take your broken pieces, your shattered heart and life to God, His restoration glows through with His healing.

Nothing is too hard for God, no life is too shattered for God, nothing is impossible for God.

God's mending, restoration, and renewal, weaves a golden bond as the goodness of God, the tender mercies of God, heals the broken-hearted and binds wounds.

Are you broken?

Become a shining one, a glowing one, by allowing God to heal your wounds and scars. Let God take what the enemy meant for evil and turn it to good. Allow God's healing, light-filled restoration to shine in you and through you. For through the broken, God's light shines.

Heavenly Father, I give my broken places to You. Shine Your light in the dark places and bring healing and restoration. Father, You promise to heal the brokenhearted and bind our wounds. Father, I can't see the good right now, I can't see a purpose in the pain, but I know that all things work together for good for those who love You and are called according to Your purpose.

Jesus, You came to preach the good news, to announce release to the captives, recovery of sight to the blind, and deliver the oppressed, downtrodden, bruised, crushed, and broken-down.

Oh, Jesus, weave Your golden bond, Your tender mercies to mend, renew, and restore so that Your healing light shines in me and through me.

God's Timeless Truth

"He heals the brokenhearted and binds up their wounds [healing their pain and comforting their sorrow]" (Psalm 147:3, AMP).

"And we know that all things work together for good for those who love God, who are called according to his purpose" (Romans 8:28, NET Bible).

"The Spirit of the Lord [is] upon Me, because He has

anointed Me [the Anointed One, the Messiah] to preach the good news (the Gospel) to the poor; He has sent Me to announce release to the captives and recovery of sight to the blind, to send forth as delivered those who are oppressed [who are downtrodden, bruised, crushed, and broken down by calamity]" (Luke 4:18, AMPC).

Making room

The new kid in town, once again boarded a bus to a new school. Uncool and scrawny, glasses that weren't fashionable, clothes that weren't stylish, she looked for a place to sit. The bus wasn't crowded, and even though the seats were made for two children, each seat had been claimed. Every child already on the bus sat near the aisle, not leaving room, not giving an inch or opportunity for this skinny new kid.

She tried to be brave, asked several if she could sit, but they just looked ahead and ignored her pleas. No one, not one, offered her a place to sit; not one person made room for her.

The bus driver finally stood to his feet and demanded one girl move over to make room for the new kid. Trembling, the new kid sat and tried to calm her heart, tried not to let a tear fall, not show how much it hurt to not be accepted or wanted. I know how she feels. I know because I was that scrawny new kid.

Life is hard when no one will make room for you -- room on the seat next to them, room for one more person, room to add a new friend in their lives. Unfortunately, it wouldn't be the last time I felt an outcast or the last time I would be a new kid in town.

As painful as that experience, and other experiences were, God used each moment of pain. He's used the pain to help me be sensitive to others and used it to draw me closer to Him.

God knows how much it hurts when rejected.

Jesus knows. He came to the earth He created, and the

people He created didn't make room for Him. Born in a stable because there wasn't room in the Inn. Rejected by men, Jesus didn't let the rejection and pain stop Him. Jesus sacrificed Himself in our place, died on a cross, rose again, and offers eternal life for all who will come, all who will make room for Him.

Jesus has made room for you and invites you in.

Will you make room for Him? Jesus holds out His loving nail-scarred hands. Will you open your heart and allow Him into Your heart?

Jesus scoots over, pats the seat next to Him, and invites you to sit with Him, live with Him, where He makes eternal room for you in His heart and in Heaven.

Jesus, thank You that Your arms are always open and Your heart is always open. Thank You for Your amazing, generous invitation to welcome all who will come to You.

God's Timeless Truth

"Look! I stand at the door and knock. If you hear my voice and open the door, I will come in, and we will share a meal together as friends. Those who are victorious will sit with me on my throne, just as I was victorious and sat with my Father on his throne" (Revelation 3:20-21, NLT).

"All whom My Father gives (entrusts) to Me will come to Me; and the one who comes to Me I will most certainly not cast out [I will never, no never, reject one of them who comes to Me]" (John 6:37, AMPC).

"If you declare with your mouth, 'Jesus is Lord,' and if you believe in your heart that God raised Jesus from the dead, you will be saved. We believe with our hearts, and so we are made right with God. And we declare with our mouths that we believe, and so we are saved. As the Scripture says, 'Anyone who trusts in him will never be disappointed'" (Romans 10:9-11, NCV).

"Then I saw a new heaven and a new earth, for the old heaven and the old earth had disappeared. And the sea was also gone. And I saw the holy city, the new Jerusalem, coming down from God out of heaven like a bride beautifully dressed for her husband. I heard a loud shout from the throne, saying, 'Look, God's home is now among his people! He will live with them, and they will be his people. God himself will be with them'" (Revelation 21:1-3, NLT).

Victory of the fallen

I've fallen and I can't get up!
There are days I feel like my soul is bleeding with gaping wounds. Concerns for friends, family, and the world claw at my back. Attacks by Satan leave me bruised, battered and weary, prayers remain unanswered, and life is just plain difficult.

In Christ, our souls are bullet-proof invincible, but we still bleed.

Trials hit hard and I hit the floor. I hit the floor on my knees and I just plain hit the floor from sadness, grief, and overwhelming circumstances. Crushed and defeated, I wondered at times if I'd ever get back up. I want things to be different, answers to come, and prayers to be answered, but they haven't. Nothing has changed yet in the situation. My prayers continue for change and for change in me.

Desperate for a word from God, desperate for a soul-revival, I fall at God's mercy and beg for His lovingkindness. "My heart is in anguish within me, and terrors ... have fallen upon me" (Psalm 55:4).

Through my heart's call, the reminder comes... "If Your law had not been my delight, then **I would have perished in my affliction**. I will never forget Your precepts, for by them **You have revived me**. I am Yours, save me; for I have sought Your precepts" (Psalm 119:92-94, NASB). **"This is my comfort and consolation in my affliction: that Your word has revived me and given me life"** (Psalm 119:50, AMPC). (Emphasis added).

The saving in afflictions comes in various forms as God's word brings revival for afflicted souls, His life bringing life.

In a world that bruises and bleeds there is One who bruised and bled to heal your bruised broken heart and mend and bind your bleeding wounds.

There is victory for the fallen. We fall on our knees at the feet of Jesus to receive His grace and mercy. For, when God's grace falls on a willing soul, the soul becomes free in Christ.

> *"Let every failure teach you to cling afresh to Christ, and He will prove Himself a mighty and a loving Helper." ~ Andrew Murray*

No matter how far one falls, God's loving arm is mighty to save, restore, and redeem, for no sin is too dark for the power of Christ to lift with His grace, healing, and mercy.

With Christ, chains fall off prisoners, scales fall off blind eyes, and oppression falls away as His Holy Spirit falls within. And, when the Holy Spirit fell on people, mighty things happened.

Christ's followers have God's Spirit living within, granting the power of God. We fall into God's arms during times of trouble, and in our fallen weakness, His strength is given. A dead seed fallen into the ground, produces new life.

As we lay down our life, surrendering self, surrendering our sorrows, troubles, and pain, The Life comes to give hope, comfort, and strength.

Have troubles fallen on your shoulders? Have you fallen? Fall into the love of Christ, to receive forgiveness, relief, grace, restoration, and help for every need. Fall on your knees, fall into God's Word, and fall into God's grace. Though you fall, His hand will hold you up, forever hold you, and forever love you.

Heavenly Father, thank You for Your unfailing love and mercy. Thank You that when I fall, You are there to put me back on my feet. Thank You when I fall on Your mercy, Your loving hand will catch me in Your grace. Thank You, Father. Thank you.

God's Timeless Truth

"Give your burdens to the Lord, and he will take care of you. He will not permit the godly to slip and fall" (Psalm 55:22, NLT).

"...get help from the God of Jacob, put your hope in God and know real blessing! ... He always does what he says— he defends the wronged, he feeds the hungry. God frees prisoners—he gives sight to the blind, he lifts up the fallen." (Psalm 146:8, MSG).

God heals the heartbroken and bandages their wounds. God puts the fallen on their feet again (Psalm 147:2-6, MSG).

"When people's steps follow the Lord, God is pleased with their ways. If they stumble, they will not fall, because the Lord holds their hand" (Psalm 37:23-24, NCV).

Back side of the desert

Sandaled feet scuffed on rocky soil, no other person in sight, no reprieve from the heat of the noonday sun, he stopped and surveyed his surroundings. At one time, he'd been a man of power and wealth, a man schooled in the finest Egypt had to offer. At one time, he thought he had a grand purpose. For forty years he'd lived in the back side of the desert, hidden from his past, a hostage of the mistake that haunted his days and nights (Exodus 2).

Now, he tended sheep. He herded and kept livestock that didn't even belong to him, he had nothing to his name other than his wife and sons. Nothing to offer anyone. He'd come to the desert and here he would stay, here he would die.

God had other ideas. God called from the burning bush not consumed by fire. From within the flames, the Voice called Moses out of the desert. The one held hostage by his failure, is called to free a people held hostage (Exodus 3).

God finds the one who thinks they have gone too far from His grace, the one who thinks they have been forgotten, the one who is hiding, the one who thinks they have no purpose.

God's love never fails to find you, to call to you, to give new mercies every morning, new hope, new plans, and new opportunities. No matter where you are, what you have done, whatever has happened to you, God's love never fails, and His love will never fail to lead you to a new beginning.

Heavenly Father, thank You that You are the one who finds those wandering in desert lands, in the howling waste of the wilderness.

Thank You that You will encircle and care for me and guard me as the pupil of Your eye. Thank You that You take scarlet sins, red as crimson, and wash them in your grace and cleanse like wool and make me white as snow (Isaiah 1:18). Thank You that You know the plans You have for me, plans for peace and well-being, and not for disaster, to give me a future and a hope (Jeremiah 29:11). Thank You that You promise to do something new, springing forth, making a road in the wilderness and rivers in the desert!

God's Timeless Truth

"He found him in a desert land, and in the howling waste of a wilderness; He encircled him, He cared for him, He guarded him as the pupil of His eye" (Deuteronomy 32:10, NASB).

"Do not remember the past events, pay no attention to things of old. Look, I am about to do something new; even now it is coming. Do you not see it? Indeed, I will make a way in the wilderness, rivers in the desert" (Isaiah 43:18-19, HCSB).

Reaching out

Concerned for a loved one in the midst of many struggles, I went to God in prayer. While I prayed, I visualized my arm reaching toward my loved one, knowing although they live far away, my prayers are not bound by distance, time, or space.

I knew my sweet husband was also praying, and I imagined my husband's arm coming over mine, reaching further toward our loved one. The verse came to mind, "For where two or three have gathered together in My name, I am there in their midst" (Matthew 18:20, NASB).

I realized, as we prayed, Jesus joined us. His strong mighty arm reached over ours grasping the hand of our loved one. My arms, and my husband's arms, cannot reach across the country or around the world, but our Heavenly Father has eternal, unfailing, limitless, all-powerful, loving arms.

We can pray for others.... Like Abraham took members of his household to rescue Lot. Like David and his soldiers went to rescue their families who were taken captive. We too can enlist members of the household of faith to pray with us for the rescue of our family members.

The enemy may try to grab at us, claw at our loved ones, but remember what Jesus said... "My sheep hear My voice, and I know them, and they follow Me; and I give eternal life to them, and they will never perish; and no one will snatch them out of My hand. My Father, who has given them to Me, is greater than all; and no one is able to snatch them out of the Father's hand" (John 10:27-29, NASB).

Reach out in prayer (as Moses did) for those who have turned from the Lord.

The Israelites had turned their backs on God, "but Moses, his chosen one, stood before him and stopped God's anger from destroying them" (Psalm 106 21, 23).
Will you stand in the gap for your loved ones, for those who are lost?
Reach out in person, reach out in love, and reach out in prayer. For, "the heartfelt and persistent prayer of a righteous man (believer) can accomplish much [when put into action and made effective by God—it is dynamic and can have tremendous power]" (James 5:16, AMP).
Reach out, friends. Keep reaching out. Your prayers are boundless and unlimited in the boundless love and unlimited power of our amazing God.

Heavenly Father, I'm reaching out in prayer for my loved one. I'm reaching out to You because Your arm is long enough and strong enough to reach anyone. Thank You that You are powerful enough and mighty enough to break through any stronghold or sin, for nothing is impossible for You. Father, please touch my loved one's life and bring them back to You.
Please bring the lost ones into Your loving presence. Open eyes blinded by the devil and melt stone hearts, so they will turn to You and receive the eternal joy of You.

God's Timeless Truth

"Behold, the Lord's hand is not so short that it cannot save; nor is His ear so dull that it cannot hear" (Isaiah 59:1, NASB).
God gently reassures, "...You are My servant, I have

chosen you and not rejected you. Do not fear, for I am with you; do not anxiously look about you, for I am your God. I will strengthen you, surely I will help you, surely I will uphold you with My righteous right hand.' Behold, all those who are angered at you will be shamed and dishonored; those who contend with you will be as nothing and will perish. You will seek those who quarrel with you, but will not find them, those who war with you will be as nothing and non-existent. For I am the Lord your God, who upholds your right hand, who says to you, 'Do not fear, ... I will help you,' declares the Lord. Your Redeemer is the Holy One of Israel. ... you will rejoice in the Lord; you will glory in the Holy One of Israel. ... I, the Lord, will answer them Myself, as the God of Israel I will not forsake them. ...That they may see and recognize, and consider and gain insight as well, that the hand of the Lord has done this, and the Holy One of Israel has created it" (Isaiah 41:9-20, NASB).

Obedient blessings

Desperate for warmth, I stood in front of our gas fireplace. Lamb wool booties on my feet, jeans, flannel shirt, a fleece robe over my clothing, and I still couldn't get warm. Our young son ran around the house with his shirt off, and I shivered and huddled as close to the fire as I could. My southern-born blood refused to adjust to the Chicagoland cold.

During our over four-year stay in the Chicago area, I begged and pleaded for God to return me to the sunny, warm, hot, sunny, warm, blissfully warm South. Yes, I really missed the sun and wanted to be warm!

In my quiet time, I clung to the verses, "Behold, I will bring them from the north country, and gather them from the ends of the earth..." (Jeremiah 31:8, NKJV).

"I will say to the north, 'Give them up!' And to the south, 'Do not hold them back.' Bring My sons from afar and My daughters from the ends of the earth" (Isaiah 43:6, NASB).

"But you will not go out in haste, nor will you go as fugitives; for the Lord will go before you, and the God of Israel will be your rear guard" (Isaiah 52:12, NASB).

One day during a time of prayer, I felt in my spirit "get your house in order, change is going to come." Hoping I heard God correctly, I fixed up the house by painting, adding wallpaper, added tile backsplash in the kitchen, installed crown molding and a chair rail, faux painted in several rooms, and added a patio.

My goal was to make the house look like a model home and be ready for whenever God would open His hopefully southern-bound door.

For over three years, I prayed, waited, watched, and worked on getting our house in order. Our son started preschool, then kindergarten, then first grade, then second grade, and the wait continued. In spite of my wimpy attitude and cold natured body; we enjoyed Chicago museums, the aquarium, and various sites around our location. God blessed with wonderful forever friends and the amazing blessing of watching our back-door neighbors being baptized.

Then, in God's perfect timing, my husband called and said his boss wanted him to move to Texas for a new job. Woo-hoo!

I hung up the phone and called the real estate agent. Our house sold the next day. Within a span of three weeks, we sold our Chicago house, flew to Texas, found a home ready for purchase, came back and moved out of our old house and into our new one.

The wait at the time seemed long (and cold), but God's plan is perfect and incredible. By being obedient in preparing the house, we were ready the moment we received the call, the transition was smooth, and the selling price higher than imagined.

Every day we are given opportunities to receive God's blessings through obedience. We may not have to move physically to achieve blessings, but we do have to be prepared to move spiritually. Obedience is a barometer of love and trust of God.

When we obey God and allow Him to work in whatever way He chooses, we might not see immediate results, yet every step forward in obedience leads to the next God-given step and the blessing of spiritual growth.

Has God whispered in your soul?

Do you have a holy nudge to step out in faith? Move forward as God leads and let your soul stretch to receive growth and blessings.

> *"He [God] delights to meet the faith of one who looks up to Him and says, 'Lord, You know that I cannot do this—but I believe that You can!"*
> ~ Amy Carmichael

Thank You, God that You are God forever and ever and You will guide me today and from now on. Help me to be obedient to listen closely to Your voice, be obedient and follow You. Thank You that through Your mighty power at work within me, You will accomplish infinitely more than I might ask or think.

> *"God wants to do the impossible through your life. All He requires is your obedience. ... God does not need you to dream great dreams for your life, your family, your business, or your church. He simply asks for obedience. He has plans that would dwarf yours in comparison.*
> ~ Henry & Richard Blackaby[iii]

God's Timeless Truth

"The Lord leads with unfailing love and faithfulness all who keep his covenant and obey his demands" (Psalm 25:10, NLT).

"This God, our God forever and ever—He will always lead us" (Psalm 48:14, HCSB).

"So, rejoice in the Lord and be glad, all you who obey him! Shout for joy, all you whose hearts are pure!" (Psalm 32:11, NLT).

"Now all glory to God, who is able, through his mighty power at work within us, to accomplish infinitely more than we might ask or think. Glory to him in the church and in Christ Jesus through all generations forever and ever! Amen" (Ephesians 3:20, NLT).

Misplaced emphasis

The Olympics showcases athletes from around the world who have trained for years, who strive to reach a goal to attain a spot on the victory podium.

Many have had minor and major injuries, some told by friends, family members, even doctors, they would never be able to compete. Yet, those who kept going, who refused to give in to their injuries, continued to move forward by keeping their eyes on the prize. Those athletes are the ones who refused to listen to the naysayers and kept the emphasis on their goal to win.

We all have that choice.

We have a choice as to what we will do, who we listen to, how we compete in this race called life. If the devil can get us to focus on the negative, we won't see the positive. If the devil can get us to think we can never get over something, then we won't move forward, and we won't allow God's healing to get us over what happened. We get stuck in the devil's trap forgetting that Jesus has made a way for Jesus Is the Way.

The emphasis has been placed on the wrong things! The devil says you can't get out, you won't find healing, you can never change, never find hope, never be able to move forward, you'll always be messed up by the mess you've endured or the mess you made.

Satan is a liar!

Negative things may scar, wound, and mess with us, but because of Jesus there is nothing done that can't be restored and renewed by the power of our all-powerful God.

> *"We are too prone to engrave our trials in marble and write our blessings in sand."*
> ~ Charles Spurgeon

The defining moments of our lives are not our hardships, traumas, and trials, but how (and if) we allow Jesus to heal our hardships, traumas, and trials.

Instead of placing the emphasis on the mess done by the devil, let's place the emphasis on the message of what God has done, who God is, what God can do no matter how messy the life. Jesus makes all things new. All things! No one is too messed up for nothing is impossible for God!

Be an overcomer, be one who allows God to change those defining moments into refining moments. Be one who keeps the eye on the eternal prize, who chooses to move forward no matter what the devil says and no matter what the devil has done. Move forward in the power of our all-powerful, healing, restoring, amazing God. And one day you will stand on the victory podium in heaven, because you overcame the devil by the blood of the Lamb and the word of your testimony (Revelation 12:11).

Father, thank You that You heal the brokenhearted and bind up my wounds, curing my pains and sorrows. Thank You that nothing is ever impossible for You and no word from You will be without power or impossible of fulfillment.

Help me to keep my eyes on Jesus who both began and finished this race. Help me to study how Jesus made it through His time on earth.

Because Jesus never lost sight of where He was headed—that exhilarating finish in and with You—He could put up with anything along the way: Cross, shame, whatever. And now He's there, in the place of honor, right alongside You.

Help me to give You all my sorrow and pain, all my broken places, so that You can heal and restore. Help me Father when I'm struggling in my faith to go over that story again, item by item, that long litany of hostility Jesus plowed through. Because that will shoot adrenaline into my soul.

Help me to focus on You and always remember all that You have done. Help me to carve my blessings in granite and my trials in the sand. For You have done amazing things and will continue to do amazing things!

God's Timeless Truth

"He heals the brokenhearted and bandages their wounds" (Psalm 147:3, NLT).
"For with God nothing is ever impossible and no word from God shall be without power or impossible of fulfillment" (Luke 1:37, AMPC).
"Keep your eyes on Jesus, who both began and finished this race we're in. Study how he did it. Because he never lost sight of where he was headed—that exhilarating finish in and with God—he could put up with anything along the way: Cross, shame, whatever. And now he's there, in the place of honor, right alongside God. When you find yourselves flagging in your faith, go over that story again, item by item, that long litany of hostility he plowed through. That will shoot adrenaline into your souls!" (Hebrews 12:2-3, MSG).

Dictated by days

Does one day define you? One thing, one person, one circumstance, one action, one trial, one tragedy, ... one day?

One day, or many days, can change the direction or focus, can change everything. However, I have good news -- trials that railroaded into our lives are switched on the track of eternal time by the loving hand of our Heavenly Father.

Our worst days are changed by the best day in history -- the day Jesus rose from the grave. The resurrection of Jesus gives hope that life will be resurrected. The days that dictated your trajectory are changed by Jesus who sets free every captive and heals every broken heart, and His grace covers every day of sin. His restoration changes every negative experience. The defining of our lives is not by what happened to us, but what happened through Jesus.

God defines you as His creation, His beloved child, for in Jesus you are loved, beloved, forgiven, restored, and renewed. No day is too messed up to be remade and redeemed by God. Jesus who is hope, comes and blesses, heals, renews, bringing eternal hope.

Whatever has happened, whatever you have done, God's grace and restoration are available.

Have you been falsely accused, beaten, or abused? Paul, Peter, most of the disciples know how you feel, and Jesus definitely knows how you feel.

Have you been a liar, thief, prodigal, denied Christ, or run from God? Ask Jacob, the thief on the cross, the prodigal son, Peter, and Jonah about the mercy and restoration of God.

Is murder too hard for God? Ask David and Moses about the grace and restoration of God.

Is adultery too hard to forgive? Ask David, the woman at the well, and the woman caught in the act of adultery, about the grace and restoration of God.

Drinking problem, greed problem, abusive issues, cheating others, adultery, sex outside of marriage, homosexuality... Paul reminds us, "Some of you were once like that. But you were cleansed; you were made holy; you were made right with God by calling on the name of the Lord Jesus Christ and by the Spirit of our God" (1 Corinthians 6:9-11, NLT).

No matter what was done to you, no matter what you have done, no matter how hard or how dark your days, God's light of grace and restoration is waiting for you.

Start today, right now, by giving your days to Jesus and those past defining days will be redefined by the saving grace and mercy of Jesus Christ.

No sin is too dark, no day, and no difficulty is too hard for God to redeem, restore, and renew.

Heavenly Father, thank You that You take sins and cleanse them white as snow, blowing them away by Your amazing grace. Jesus, thank You for Your gentle, humble heart that takes my burdens and give my soul eternal rest. Thank You that You came to bring the Good News, to set captives free, to open blind eyes, to set free those who are oppressed, downtrodden, bruised and crushed by tragedy. Thank You that You will punish the evil for their evil deeds, and You take everything the enemy meant for evil in the lives of Your children and turn it into good.

Thank You that in You I am a new creation. The old has gone and the new has come in You! Thank You, Father!

God's Timeless Truth

Jesus said, "The Spirit of the Lord is upon me, for he has anointed me to bring Good News to the poor. He has sent me to proclaim that captives will be released, that the blind will see, that the oppressed will be set free, and that the time of the Lord's favor has come." ... "Come to me, all of you who are weary and carry heavy burdens, and I will give you rest. Take my yoke upon you. Let me teach you, because I am humble and gentle at heart, and you will find rest for your souls" (Luke 4:18-19, NLT), (Matthew 11:28-29, NLT).

"And we know that God causes all things to work together for good to those who love God, to those who are called according to His purpose" (Romans 8:28, NASB).

"The Lord says, 'Come, let us talk about these things. Though your sins are like scarlet, they can be as white as snow. Though your sins are deep red, they can be white like wool" (Isaiah 1:18, NCV).

"I have swept away your sins like a big cloud; I have removed your sins like a cloud that disappears into the air. Come back to me because I saved you" (Isaiah 44:22, NCV).

"Therefore, if anyone is in Christ, he is a new creation; old things have passed away, and look, new things have come" (2 Corinthians 5:17, HCSB).

How far will it go?

Have you ever hesitated to do something because you didn't think the impact would be worth the effort or would last? Or, you worked at something and didn't see a return for all the time and money you invested?

I wonder, how far will we go when we don't know how far our efforts will go? Will we give what little we have to God, trusting that He will take our small offering and make something amazing?

Many times, I wonder if what I offer will make a difference. I wonder if the time spent, the love given, the effort made, will be of any worth and go any distance. Yet, then I remember all things are possible with God, and our God does exceedingly, abundantly more than we ask or imagine.

While at the home of Simon the Leper, a woman brought an Alabaster vial of costly perfume to anoint Jesus. The disciples complained about using such an expensive item instead of selling the vial to use the money for the poor. However, Jesus responded to let her alone for what she had done was good. And, that wherever the gospel would be preached, the woman's sacrifice would be shared (Mark 4:3-9).

A poor widow put in the offering two small copper coins. Jesus, "calling His disciples to Him, He said to them, 'Truly I say to you, this poor widow put in more than all the contributors to the treasury; for they all put in out of their surplus, but she, out of her poverty, put in all she owned, all she had to live on.'"

What is done for God is noticed and appreciated by God.

Two thousand years ago, a crowd of people came to Jesus. When Jesus looked up and saw a great crowd coming toward Him, He asked Philip, *Where shall we buy bread for these people to eat?*

Jesus asked only to test him, for He already had in mind what He was going to do. Philip answered saying that *it would take more than half a year's wages to buy enough bread for each one to have a bite!*

Another of His disciples, Andrew, Simon Peter's brother, spoke up, *Here's a boy with five small barley loaves and two small fish, but how far will they go among so many?*

Jesus took the small offering, gave thanks, and distributed enough food for 5000 men along with women and children. And, twelve baskets were left over.

What is given to Jesus is always resurrected, transformed, recreated, made new, and multiplied in wonderful ways.

Give God what you have, give Him your love, give Him your life, and watch the amazing things, the incredible ways God will use what you offer Him.

Heavenly Father, help me to remember what is impossible for mere humans is possible for You. Thank You that You are able to do more amazing things than I can imagine.

You promise that if we give, it will be given in a good measure, pressed down, shaken together, running over, poured into our laps. For the measure I use will be the measure I receive.

Thank You that You notice and appreciate everything we do for You.

God's Timeless Truth

Jesus replied, "What is impossible with man is possible with God" (Luke 18:27, NIV).

"Give, and it will be given to you: A good measure, pressed down, shaken together, running over, will be poured into your lap. For the measure you use will be the measure you receive" (Luke 6:38, NET Bible).

"Now to Him who is able to do far more abundantly beyond all that we ask or think, according to the power that works within us, to Him be the glory in the church and in Christ Jesus to all generations forever and ever. Amen" (Ephesians 3:20, NASB).

Hope is born

In the darkness, into the chaos, hope comes. The dark sky split as angels proclaimed good news of great joy for all the people; for in the city of David, a Savior, Christ the Lord was born.

For God so loved the world, that He gave His only begotten Son, so that whoever believed in Him would not perish, but have eternal life.

Hope is born. Immanuel, God with us. A child born to us, a son given to us; and the government rests on His shoulders; and His name is Wonderful Counselor, Mighty God, Eternal Father, Prince of Peace. Joy to the world, the Lord is born.

Hope is born. A new day dawns with new mercies. The Word became flesh and His glory shines in the darkness, the true light lights the world, and those who receive Him become children of God.

Hope is born. Hope is born for you, in you, forever with you, forever for you, never to leave or forsake you. Father to the fatherless, defender of widows and orphans, mender of the brokenhearted, sight restorer, hope restorer, Jesus comes.

In the storm, Jesus says "Come."

To the one sick and hurting, Jesus says "Come" to His healing and restoration.

To the one needing hope, Jesus says "Come" to His soul-filling, life eternal.

Come to Jesus, come to His love, come to His eternal hope.

Christ Jesus is your hope. This hope is an anchor of the

soul, a hope both sure and steadfast. Blessed be the God and Father of our Lord Jesus Christ, who according to His great mercy has caused you to be born again to a living hope through the resurrection of Jesus Christ from the dead. For you, for forever, hope is born.

Heavenly Father, thank You for the gift of Jesus Christ and His mercy and grace. Thank You that the joy of Jesus Christ comes with Your eternal hope. Thank You that through Jesus we are given forgiveness and right standing with You. Thank You that Your hope is always present, always with us, to help us through every day through all eternity.

God's Timeless Truth

"Behold, the virgin shall be with child and shall bear a Son, and they shall call His name Immanuel,' which translated means, 'God with us' (Matthew 1:23).

"For a child will be born to us, a son will be given to us; and the government will rest on His shoulders; and His name will be called Wonderful Counselor, Mighty God, Eternal Father, Prince of Peace" (Isaiah 9:6).

At the birth of Jesus, the angel said to the shepherds, 'Do not be afraid; for behold, I bring you good news of great joy which will be for all the people; for today in the city of David there has been born for you a Savior, who is Christ the Lord" (Luke 2:10-11).

"For God so loved the world, that He gave His only begotten Son, that whoever believes in Him shall not perish, but have eternal life" (John 3:16).

"And the Word became flesh, and dwelt among us, and we saw His glory, glory as of the only begotten from the Father, full of grace and truth" (John 1:14).

"...Christ Jesus (the Messiah), our Hope" (1 Timothy 1:1).

"Praised (honored, blessed) be the God and Father of our Lord Jesus Christ (the Messiah)! By His boundless mercy we have been born again to an ever-living hope through the resurrection of Jesus Christ from the dead" (1 Peter 1:3, AMPC).

"[Now] we have this [hope] as a sure and steadfast anchor of the soul [it cannot slip and it cannot break down under whoever steps out upon it—a hope] that reaches farther and enters into [the very certainty of the Presence] ..." (Hebrews 6:19).

All verses NASB unless otherwise noted.

What are you going to do?

What are you going to do about the thing you don't like, the person you don't like, the political party and politician you don't like, the world you don't like – what are you going to do? You have a choice. Complain, be angry, post negativity on social media, whine, mope, crawl in a hole, never leave your house, never leave your church group, not even go to church?

Satan wants us to do nothing and hide so that he can continue making a mess of an already messy world. Negativity sucks the soul into a whirlwind of negativity.

The less positive change is made, the less positive change will come. We can focus and complain about what is not liked, what we wish would change, or we can focus on God, who is love, who can change anything and everything with His love.

Positive change comes in our lives, and the lives of others, when we love God, love others, go, tell others about God, make disciples, and love with God's love.

Your life, the time you spend with God, makes a difference. Your prayers make a difference. You may not be able to change the world, change everyone else, but you can be the change.

Leave the world a better place because you loved with God's love while you were in the world.

What are you going to do?

Father, thank You for Your love. Please help me to love You with all my heart, and with all my soul, and with all my mind, and with all my strength, and love my neighbor as myself.

Change me to be more like You so that I may be used by You. Help me to filter my thoughts through Your love, my words through Your love, and my actions through Your love. Let all I do be done through Your love so that Your love pours forth. You are the One the world needs and You are the change the world needs.

God's Timeless Truth

"Here is a simple rule of thumb for behavior: Ask yourself what you want people to do for you; then grab the initiative and do it for them! If you only love the lovable, do you expect a pat on the back? Run-of-the-mill sinners do that. If you only help those who help you, do you expect a medal? Garden-variety sinners do that. If you only give for what you hope to get out of it, do you think that's charity? The stingiest of pawnbrokers does that.
"I tell you, love your enemies. Help and give without expecting a return. You'll never—I promise—regret it. Live out this God-created identity the way our Father lives toward us, generously and graciously, even when we're at our worst. Our Father is kind; you be kind.
"Don't pick on people, jump on their failures, criticize their faults—unless, of course, you want the same treatment. Don't condemn those who are down; that hardness can boomerang. Be easy on people; you'll find life a lot easier. Give away your life; you'll find life given back, but not merely given back—given back with bonus and blessing. Giving, not getting, is the way. Generosity begets generosity" (Luke 6:31-38, MSG).

Prayer CPR

Slumped at the kitchen table, I fought an illness that had lasted for weeks. Then at 9:48 that morning, I felt a surge in my spirit as the pain lifted. I knew without a doubt God had moved. And within my spirit, came a realization someone had prayed, someone had brought me before God's throne.

A few days later, when I couldn't breathe, couldn't catch my breath when some unexpected, soul-shattering news came, I knew again at 4:13 pm someone prayed. Their prayers breathed grace, life support for breath when life is too hard and breath couldn't come on its own.

I'm grateful for those who pray. Who feel the gentle nudge to pray, who don't ignore God's prompting, who battle in the heavenlies for those in need.

Your prayers make a difference.

Your prayers provide heavenly CPR, God's grace breathing into others who need life support. Your prayers are the oxygen mask for those struggling to breathe during difficult events.

Please pray when the Holy Spirit prompts you to pray. When God's spirit moves, move in action, move right then, for someone may not be able to stand and needs your prayer support. Breathe grace through your prayers, for your prayers drop mercy drops on those who are hurting.

Please pray.

Father, thank You that I can come to You in prayer. Please help me to pray. Help me when Your Holy Spirit brings someone to mind, gently nudges me to pray, to pray right then.

Help me to pray in the Spirit at all times and on every occasion to stay alert and be persistent in my prayers for all believers everywhere (Ephesians 6:18, NLT).

> *"Prayer for another person is like touching God with one hand and touching the person with the other. That's what intercessory prayer is all about."* ~ Jim Cymbala

God's Timeless Truth

"Be unceasing and persistent in prayer" (1 Thessalonians 5:17, AMP).

"For there is no distinction between Jew and Gentile; for the same Lord is Lord over all [of us], and [He is] abounding in riches (blessings) for all who call on Him [in faith and prayer]" (Romans 10:12, AMP).

Pray as Moses did when he interceded for the Israelites (Exodus 32:7-14, Numbers 11:2, Numbers 21:7).

Pray for your brothers and sisters in Christ like those who prayed for Paul. "While you join in helping us by your prayers. Then thanks will be given by many persons on our behalf for the gracious gift [of deliverance] granted to us through the prayers of many [believers]." ...

"At the same time pray for us, too, that God will open a door [of opportunity] to us for the word, to proclaim the mystery of Christ, for which I have been imprisoned." ... "Brothers and sisters, pray for us." "Finally, brothers and sisters, pray continually for us that the word of the Lord will spread rapidly and be honored [triumphantly celebrated and glorified], just as it was with you" (2 Corinthians 1:11,

Colossians 4:3, 1 Thessalonians 5:25, 2 Thessalonians 3:1, AMP).

Remember, "The heartfelt and persistent prayer of a righteous man (believer) can accomplish much [when put into action and made effective by God—it is dynamic and can have tremendous power]" (James 5:16, AMP).

Pray. Please pray.

Acid

My ear throbbed and ached, and relief was nowhere to be found. The doctor prescribed an antibiotic, yet the pain continued. My tolerance for pain is extremely high, and I was sure the inside of my ear must be bleeding profusely as the eardrum vibrated with agony. Worst. Ear. Infection. Ever!

I mentioned the problem to a church friend, and she shared about a time her ears had been infected due to acid reflux backing up in her ear canal. I didn't even know that could happen.

Reading about the problem helped me discover that acid reflux is often caused by eating and then lying down shortly after a meal. Sitting up helps keep the digestive juices from slipping into the esophagus, throat, and at times into the ear canal.

I now try to avoid eating for several hours before bedtime and make sure to keep upright so the digestive process can properly work. My esophagus, throat, and ear canals have been much happier.

I wonder how many people are nibbling away on sin, lying down in sin, thinking no harm will come? Sin is like acid reflux, eating away, infecting, destroying, and causing agony. No sin is just a "little" sin; every sin comes with a negative consequence.

However, there is good news. The love of Jesus Christ covers sin with His grace for those who come seeking His mercy.

Got sin? Jesus is the cure and relief for sin agony. Jesus Christ heals, restores, and grants new life.

Heavenly Father, help me not to lie down in any sin but to quickly run to You for forgiveness. Thank You for Your grace and mercy that sets me free!

God's Timeless Truth

"When I kept silent about my sin, my body wasted away through my groaning all day long" (Psalm 32:3, NASB).

"When you were spiritually dead because of your sins and because you were not free from the power of your sinful self, God made you alive with Christ, and he forgave all our sins. For He rescued us from the domain of darkness and transferred us to the kingdom of His beloved Son, in whom we have redemption, the forgiveness of sins" (Colossians 2:13, NCV), Colossians 1:13-14, NASB).

"How happy he is whose wrong doing is forgiven, and whose sin is covered! How happy is the man whose sin the Lord does not hold against him..." (Psalm 32:1-2, NLV).

Dwelling in the shadow of His wings

Like a tiny screeching fire-alarm, Tinnitus rings in my skull. The noise is getting worse, louder, more distracting, so loud that sleep has become difficult. A fan whirs in our bedroom, next to me a sound machine mimics falling rain, but neither can drown out, and nothing stops the shrieking noise from ear damage.

I try to focus beyond the sound, look to God, force my mind to pray and praise, to concentrate beyond the constant maddening noise. The times I'm successful, peace and sleep bring blessed relief.

Life is full of difficult distractions screaming and screeching for attention. Help is very needed to help make it through. Psalm 91 gives hope, **"He who dwells in the shelter of the Most High will abide in the shadow of the Almighty. ... He will cover you with His pinions, and under His wings you may seek refuge."** The word "dwelling" in the original Hebrew means to sit, remain, and stay.

Dwelling in God's shelter is a decision, choice, and focus. Every moment, we are given a choice to remain and stay in the shelter of God where we are blessed to abide in His shadow, safe under the refuge of His wings.

How does this look in the craziness and screeching noise of everyday life? Fortunately, Jesus is our perfect example. Even though life was messy and hard while Jesus walked this earth, He kept focused on His Heavenly Father.

Jesus did as God directed, He went about doing good, healing, feeding, teaching, performing miracles, and proclaiming the Good News.

Even when faced with the cross, Jesus's focus remained steadfast for the "joy set before Him" (Hebrews 12:2).

The joy of Jesus was beyond the cross. He came, died and rose again, to be a perfect sacrifice of God's grace and mercy to offer all who would accept His hope, joy, peace, and eternal life. Jesus walked in the shadow of His Father, and we too can walk in the shadow of the grace of our Father and Savior, Jesus Christ.

True life is beyond this life. Earth is not your true home, you're only passing through, and amazing things await at the finish line in heaven. You are here for this time, to make an impact for all eternity.

Dwell in the shadow of God's wings, sheltered in His refuge, and for the joy set before you, press forward, reach for the upward calling to share the good news. Run your race, keep your eye on the eternal prize, show yourself approved as a workman for Jesus Christ; be about your Heavenly Father's business, for a joy-filled eternal crown awaits.

Heavenly Father, thank You that You are our help and in the shadow of Your wings I will rejoice. Thank You that You will make known to us the path of life. Thank You that in Your presence we are given fullness of joy and at Your right hand there are pleasures forever.

Help me to set my mind and keep focused on the heavenly things above, not on the temporary things on the earth. Thank You that my new, real life is hidden with Christ in God, and one day I will be in the glorious presence of my Savior.

God's Timeless Truth

"How precious is Your lovingkindness, O God! Therefore, the children of men put their trust under the shadow of Your wings" (Psalm 36:7, NKJV).

"May the Lord reward your work, and your wages be full from the Lord, the God of Israel, under whose wings you have come to seek refuge" (Ruth 2:12, NASB).

"Keep me as the apple of Your eye; hide me in the shadow of Your wings" (Psalm 17:8, NASB).

"Let me dwell in Your tent forever; let me take refuge in the shelter of Your wings" (Psalm 61:4, NASB).

"For You have been my help, and in the shadow of Your wings I sing for joy" (Psalm 63:7, NASB).

Turning the prayers

A friend sent an email to her prayer partners and suggested taking a few days to not ask God for anything but instead spend that time thanking and praising Him. I wondered, what would that look like? How could that be done when there are so many needs?

I thought of a friend I visit. I know she loves me, no doubt. However, during visits to her house, she stayed busy. She talked to me, enjoyed my company, but she kept cleaning, or straightening, or the television stayed on, there wasn't a moment of silence where we could talk in a quiet environment, sit quietly together, and just enjoy one another's presence.

I thought of another friend who never called unless she had a problem. She wouldn't call to tell me anything good in her life. Instead, her calls were complaints, worries, and concerns, then she would ask me to pray for her, and off she would go with her life.

I hate to admit, I have been that kind of friend with God. I've stayed busy and distracted during times of prayer. I've called on God over and over with my complaints, worries and concerns, then trotted off to go about my day.

How often have I come into God's presence just to say hello, tell Him I love Him, and thank Him for who He is and all He has done?

I want to do better, to change my prayers, and pray in a way that blesses and honors God.

The Psalmist reminds us to... "Know (perceive, recognize, and understand with approval) that the Lord is God! It is He Who has made us, not we ourselves [and we are

His]! We are His people and the sheep of His pasture. Enter into His gates with thanksgiving and a thank offering and into His courts with praise! Be thankful and say so to Him, bless and affectionately praise His name! For the Lord is good; His mercy and loving-kindness are everlasting, His faithfulness and truth endure to all generations" (Psalm 100:3-5, AMPC).

The wonderful thing is, even with our real-life concerns, we can pray in a praising and thankful manner.

The more we turn our prayers from complaints to praise and thanksgiving, the more peace floods the soul, the more encouragement (and courage) is given, the stronger our hope becomes, and the more our faith grows.

Thank God today. Thank God for today. Thank God that even when the world seems out of control, He is always in control. Thank God and praise Him that even when our loved ones are lost or straying that God is the One who searches (and finds) lost sheep. Praise and thank God that we can cast our burdens on the Lord for He cares for us.

Praise God that His mercies, grace, and forgiveness are new every morning. Thank God that He takes what the enemy meant for evil and turns it into good. Praise God that He is the God who heals, restores, and redeems.

Whatever you are facing, whatever worry and concern you may have, whatever burden you may carry, thank and praise God that He is a loving and compassionate God and nothing is impossible for Him.

Will you join me in turning your prayers into times of thanking and praising God?

Heavenly Father, thank You. I love You! Thank You for Your unfailing love, mercy, and grace.

Thank You for the sacrifice of Your Son, Jesus Christ. Thank You for searching for me when I was lost and finding me. Thank You for opening Your loving arms to me. Praise You that You are wonderful, awesome, and holy. Thank You for the privilege and honor of being Yours and being able to come into Your presence with my prayers.

Father, thank You that nothing is impossible for You. Thank You that my loved one is not too lost for You to find. Thank You that You know my every need and promise to meet all our needs. Thank You that You are with us in the difficulties of life and promise to help us through every difficulty. And one day, I will be in Your presence forever in heaven. Thank You, Father! I praise You! I love You!

God's Timeless Truth

"Serve the Lord with gladness; come before His presence with singing" (Psalm 100:2, NKJV).

"Enter into His gates with thanksgiving, and into His courts with praise. Be thankful to Him and bless His name. For the Lord is good; His mercy is everlasting, and His truth endures to all generations" (Psalm 100:4-5, NKJV).

"Let us come before His presence with thanksgiving; let us shout joyfully to Him with psalms" (Psalm 95:2, NKJV).

What will we miss?

Have you ever wanted to go somewhere, perhaps even been invited to go somewhere, but because of insecurity, or being too tired or unsure of the invitation, you hesitated and missed the opportunity? I've missed many, and later regretted I didn't take a leap of faith.

God brought the Israelites out of Egypt, out of slavery, to bring them to a wonderful opportunity in a new land. However, their fear caused them to hesitate and refuse to take what God had offered. Instead of getting God's best, they wandered in the desert for forty years.

God's offers are always the best. They may not be the easiest, but they are always the best. He often asks us to step out of our comfort zones to reveal new and exciting adventures.

God has no limits and His resources, power, strength, and might are inexhaustible. As we venture outside of our own ideas, thoughts, reasoning, and insecurities, we are blessed to watch the amazing ways God works.

Do you feel a Holy Spirit nudge to step out in faith with God? Please don't miss what God offers.

Please don't miss the adventure that waits when you whole-heartedly follow Him. Step out with Him and watch what He will do!

Heavenly Father, I'm stepping out to step closer to You. I don't want to miss anything You have for me. Help me to faithfully follow You.

Please forgive me when I look at things from what I think I can accomplish, instead of remembering You do more than I could ever ask or imagine. Help me to walk by faith, not by my limited sight.

Oh, Father, I don't want to miss a thing You have planned in Your perfect planning. Help me to stay focused on You and remember You do amazing things!

God's Timeless Truth

"Make me know Your ways, O Lord; teach me Your paths. Lead me in Your truth and teach me, For You are the God of my salvation; For You I wait all the day. You will make known to me the path of life; in Your presence is fullness of joy; in Your right hand there are pleasures forever. ... You enlarge my steps under me, and my feet have not slipped. The steps of a man are established by the Lord, and He delights in his way" (Psalm 25:4-5, Psalm 16:11, Psalm 18:36, Psalm 37:23, NASB).

"If we [claim to] live by the [Holy] Spirit, we must also walk by the Spirit [with personal integrity, godly character, and moral courage—our conduct empowered by the Holy Spirit]" (Galatians 5:25, AMP).

"For He whom God has sent speaks the words of God [proclaiming the Father's own message]; for God gives the [gift of the] Spirit without measure [generously and boundlessly]!" (John 3:34, AMP).

"Never lagging behind in diligence; aglow in the Spirit, enthusiastically serving the Lord; constantly rejoicing in hope [because of our confidence in Christ], steadfast and patient in distress, devoted to prayer [continually seeking wisdom, guidance, and strength]" (Romans 12:11-12, AMP).

"[Not in your own strength] for it is God Who is all the

while effectually at work in you [energizing and creating in you the power and desire], both to will and to work for His good pleasure and satisfaction and delight" (Philippians 2:13, AMPC).

Celebrating holidays

Loved ones are no longer with us, the days are shorter, darker, and colder. The Christmas season says celebrate, but it's hard sometimes, difficult to even think about decorating and celebrating. I didn't get out our regular tree. I bought a tiny one to sit on a table in the family room representing only a snippet of Christmas.

As I pondered the holidays, I remembered it's not about who is not with us, or what we have or don't have, it's about Who is with us; Immanuel – God with us -- and what He has given us --- eternal life, unfailing love, peace, hope, and joy. Therefore, I've decorated inside and outside the house. I decorated and hummed Christmas songs as I celebrated the true meaning of Christmas, the true reason to celebrate the holidays. Christ is with us which means our joy, our reason to celebrate, is always with us.

Celebrate the truth, the reality, of a God who loved you so very much, that He sent His Son to rescue you. Jesus willingly laid down His life, to die for your sins, He rose again, and opened His nail-scarred hands to welcome you into His forever family.

Celebrate the beauty of God's unfailing love. No matter how alone you may be, or how you may feel, regardless of your circumstances, you are never alone with Christ living in your heart.

We've been given eternal life in Christ; the joy of heaven came from heaven to bless us with His joy.

In Christ, we have peace that remains, for we live in an eternal kingdom. In Christ, we are given a living hope that never leaves us hopeless.

Regardless of the calendar, no matter what life holds, you are always held securely in the love of Christ. Will you join me in celebrating?

Heavenly Father, thank You that You are always with me. Thank You that even when I'm without people around me, Your loving presence is always here. Father, You know heartache and pain, and You promise comfort. Thank You that one day all tears will be wiped away and all pain removed. Thank You that I can come into Your loving, comforting presence. Thank You for Your ever-present, unfailing love.

God's Timeless Truth

"The angel said to them, 'Do not be afraid; for behold, I bring you good news of great joy which will be for all the people; for today in the city of David there has been born for you a Savior, who is Christ the Lord. ...And suddenly there appeared with the angel a multitude of the heavenly host praising God and saying, 'Glory to God in the highest, and on earth peace among men with whom He is pleased'" (Luke 2:10-14, NASB).
"All praise to God, the Father of our Lord Jesus Christ. It is by his great mercy that we have been born again, because God raised Jesus Christ from the dead. Now we live with great expectation" (1 Peter 1:3, NLT).
"Always be full of joy in the Lord. I say it again—rejoice! Let everyone see that you are considerate in all you do. Remember, the Lord is coming soon. Don't worry about anything; instead, pray about everything. Tell God what you

need and thank him for all he has done. Then you will experience God's peace, which exceeds anything we can understand. His peace will guard your hearts and minds as you live in Christ Jesus" (Philippians 4:4-7, NLT).

Always wagging

I want to be like my friend's dog. The cute little guy had been through some tough things, but now he lives with my friend. He's one happy pup, very happy to have been rescued, and every time I see him, he is wagging.

Sometimes his tail moves in a slow, steady wag. When super-joyful, he has a fast-super-happy wag. He loves his new master and he is so happy to be with her.

Why am I not like that every day with my Savior? Why isn't my life a happy wag to show the world I was rescued, I was saved, and my Master is SO VERY good!

How can you rejoice in God today? Will you show Him (and others) how happy you are to be saved?

Let's make sure we keep our life wagging with joy for Jesus!

Thank You, God for the indescribable gift of Your mercy. May my life be a free-will offering to You, joyfully serving, and rejoicing always in You. I will rejoice in the Lord and again I will rejoice!

God's Timeless Truth

"Oh, give thanks to the Lord, call upon His name; make known His deeds among the peoples." ... O give thanks to the Lord, for He is good; for His lovingkindness is everlasting" (1 Chronicles 16:8, 1 Chronicles 16:34, NASB).

"Rejoice in the Lord always; again, I will say, rejoice!" (Philippians 4:4, NASB).

"Thanks be to God for His indescribable gift!" (2

Corinthians 9:15, NASB).

"Let us give thanks all the time to God through Jesus Christ. Our gift to Him is to give thanks. Our lips should always give thanks to His name" (Hebrews 13:15, NLV).

He makes a way

"Thus says the Lord, who makes a way through the sea and a path through the mighty waters" (Isaiah 43:16, NASB).

The Egyptian chariots filled with warriors pursued the Israelites. Trapped at the Red Sea, the Israelites trembled in fear with no way forward and no way back.

However, God is the God who makes a way. He made a way through the sea, a path through the mighty waters, and He saved His people (Exodus 14).

Surrounded by enemy forces, Elisha's servant is panicked wondering what they can do. Elisha answers, "Do not fear, for those who are with us are more than those who are with them."

Then Elisha prayed, "O Lord, I pray, open his eyes that he may see." And the Lord opened the servant's eyes and he saw; and behold, the mountain was full of horses and chariots of fire all around Elisha" (2 Kings 6:16-17 NASB). Surrounded by horses and chariots, the odds impossible, but when eyes were opened to the truth, God's armies were revealed standing ready to make a way (2 Kings 6). God always makes a way.

God made a way for three Hebrew young men to be saved even in the midst of a fiery furnace (Daniel 3). God always makes a way.

A giant taunted the Israelites, made them weak-kneed and afraid, but God gave victory using one small boy with a slingshot (1 Samuel 17). God always makes a way.

God makes a way through the sunless valley. "Even though I walk through the [sunless] valley of the shadow of death, I fear no evil, for You are with me; Your rod [to protect] and Your staff [to guide], they comfort and console me" (Psalm 23:4, AMP).

Perhaps you are in the seas of trouble, the mighty wars of persecutions, financial needs, people difficulties, and life difficulties, please remember God always makes a way.

> *"My Lord Jesus is equal to every emergency. My Lord Jesus can meet the wants of every soul."*
> ~ Andrew Murray

God makes a way through the wilderness bringing rivers in the desert of our souls, our finances, and our lives. God makes a way through our past into our future.

He sets the prisoner free, forgives, redeems, restores, renews, and heals the brokenhearted.

God makes a grace-filled way for the prodigal to come home. He restores sight to those blinded by the enemy. For the repentant heart, God's mercy has removed the transgressions as far as East is from West.

Whatever you see in your way, remember God has, and will, make a way!

Heavenly Father, thank You that You always make a way, for nothing is impossible for You. Help me to remember the amazing ways You have rescued people in the past and remember all the ways You provide for those who love You.

Regardless of what I see with my eyes or experience in my life, help me to always remember that You will always make a way. Thank you, Father!

God's Timeless Truth

"Be strong and courageous, do not be afraid or tremble at them, for the Lord your God is the one who goes with you. He will not fail you or forsake you" (Deuteronomy 31:6, NASB).

"Have I not commanded you? Be strong and courageous! Do not tremble or be dismayed, for the Lord your God is with you wherever you go" (Joshua 1:9, NASB).

"The steps of a man are established by the Lord, and He delights in his way. When he falls, he will not be hurled headlong, because the Lord is the One who holds his hand" (Psalm 37:23-24, NASB).

"God arms me with strength, and He makes my way perfect. He makes me as surefooted as a deer, enabling me to stand on mountain heights. He trains my hands for battle; He strengthens my arm to draw a bronze bow. You have given me Your shield of victory. Your right hand supports me; Your help has made me great. You have made a wide path for my feet to keep them from slipping" (Psalm 18:32-36, NLT).

"Thus says the Lord, Who makes a way through the sea and a path through the mighty waters... Do not call to mind the former things or ponder things of the past. Behold, I will do something new, now it will spring forth; will you not be aware of it? I will even make a roadway in the wilderness, rivers in the desert" (Isaiah 43:16-19, NASB).

Empty to full

Jeremiah 2:5 tells of people who went far from God and "walked after emptiness and became empty." The people didn't pursue God and were left void of God, empty in mind, heart, body, and soul. I've had empty days wasting my time on worthless and futile pursuits. I've wasted hours scrolling through social media, or watching television programs, that only left me feeling empty.

However, when I spend time in Bible study or in prayer, I walk away filled and full of the goodness of God.

Jesus came to give us abundant life filled with His joy. (John 10:10, John 15:11). Paul tells us the love of Christ surpasses knowledge and fills to "all the fullness of God." Jesus is the fullness who "fills all in all" (Ephesians 3:19, 1:23). Through Christ, we are blessed with the amazing, loving, joy-filled gift of the fullness of God. Wow!

The one who can save a soul, and fill a soul, is Jesus. And with Jesus in our lives, we are blessed to produce kingdom fruit. "I am the vine, you are the branches; he who abides in Me and I in him, he bears much fruit" (John 15:5).

As Christians we are called the Bride of Christ (Revelation 19:7). We are blessed with an intimate relationship with God through Christ. We were made by Joy for joy. Not just a little joy, but full, abundant joy. Therefore, let's be like the disciples who were "continually filled with joy and with the Holy Spirit" (Acts 13:52).

No need to ever feel empty. Abide *in* Jesus, abide *with* Jesus, and you will be filled to the full with His abundant fruit-producing, life-giving joy.

Heavenly Father, thank You that I never need to feel empty when Jesus is in my life. Help me to remember to spend time with You, abide in Your presence; for in Your presence is fullness of joy. Fill me up with You!

God's Timeless Truth

"In Your presence is fullness of joy; In Your right hand there are pleasures forever" (Psalm 16:11b, NASB).

"My mouth is filled with Your praise and with Your glory all day long" (Psalm 71:8, NASB).

"Blessed are those who hunger and thirst for righteousness, for they will be filled" (Matthew 5:6, NIV).

"Let them give thanks to the Lord for His lovingkindness, and for His wonders to the sons of men! For He has satisfied the thirsty soul, and the hungry soul He has filled with what is good" (Psalm 107:8-9, NASB).

Never too far gone

Hair-raising cries echoed through the countryside. No horror movie could match the reality of the man who lived in the tombs. Reeking of blood, dirt, and stench, the naked man screeched, cut himself, and broke through chains and shackles. Driven by demons to the desert, through the mountains, to the graveyard, tormented and possessed by a legion of demons (Mark 5:1-20).

How many tried in their own effort to help him, to save him, to save themselves from him? How long had this man lived in torment? How many tears were shed for the man? How many tears were shed in fear of the man?

Was a mother praying for her son? Did she beg God night after night, day after day? Had she lost hope?

Jesus never turned away a praying parent, nor turned away those who came seeking His help. Jesus even came to those who weren't asking for help, even someone possessed by a legion of demons. A Roman legion consisted of about 5000 men. Was this man possessed by 5000 demons?

No demon, no amount of demons, can stand up to the might and authority of Jesus Christ. Jesus freed the man, gave him a right mind, clothed and restored him. No power on earth can stop the power of Jesus.

Who are you praying for? Who do you know who is chained, overwhelmed, living in the tombs of disobedience and sin? Who seems too far gone and beyond hope?

Bring them to Jesus.

No person is too far gone for Jesus. Nothing is greater than our God and nothing is impossible for God.

Pray and bring them to Jesus.

Heavenly Father, I bring _____ to You. They need You; they need freedom in You. Jesus, You tell us prayer and sometimes fasting is needed (Mark 9:29). James reminds us that the prayer of a righteous person can accomplish much, is highly effective, dynamic in power (James 5:15-16).

Father, You broke the chains of Peter in prison (Acts 12:6-7), You set the prisoners free (Acts 5:18-19), You shake the ground, unchain the prisoners, and open jail doors (Acts 16:25-26). You shut the mouths of lions (Daniel 6:16-21).

God, _____ is chained by the enemy and the devil is seeking to devour them (1 Peter 5:8). Jesus, the Father has given You all authority in heaven and earth (Matthew 28:18). Jesus, in Your name I ask that You please release _____ from their chains and release them from the devil's control. Create in them a clean heart and renew a right spirit within them (Psalm 51:10). Take away the heart of stone and give them a heart of flesh so that they may walk in Your ways (Ezekiel 11:19-20).

You search for the lost sheep and bring them home rejoicing (Luke 15:4-7). No lost person is too lost for You. Jesus, I ask that You find _____, a lost sheep, and set them free.

Oh Father, wrap them in Your love so they will forever be enraptured by Your love.

When they are brought back by You, we will all rejoice. Thank You, Father. Thank You. I ask these things in the name of Jesus Christ, who is my Savior. Amen.

God's Timeless Truth

"The Spirit of the Lord is upon Me, because He anointed Me to preach the gospel to the poor. He has sent Me to proclaim release to the captives, and recovery of sight to the blind, to set free those who are oppressed" (Luke 4:18, NASB).

"Did I not say to you that if you believe, you will see the glory of God?" (John 11:40).

"He brought them out of darkness and the shadow of death and broke their chains in pieces. Oh, that men would give thanks to the Lord for His goodness, and for His wonderful works to the children of men!" (Psalm 107:14-15, NKJV).

The mama kit miracle

Five hundred kits had been assembled and prepared for women to deliver their babies at a hospital. These birthing kits with simple supplies like a plastic sheet, string, and razor blade, are items they must have, or the hospital will not allow them use of the facility.

The Lulu Tree team met together on two acres of land God had provided for the ministry. The land where now stood a dorm for teen mothers.

Five big white tents and 500 hundred plastic chairs for the guests waited for the women. Monday morning the mamas began arriving at 9 a.m. and they didn't stop coming until 3:00 that afternoon. The steady flow of pregnant women – many teenagers, some in hijab scarves, some wearing rosaries – had been invited by local pastors.

The number of women seeking help swelled to 800 along with village children who came hungry. The team only had enough mama kits and food for 500, but the team asked God to multiply what had been brought.

The Lulu Tree founder, Emily Theresa, wrote *"And He did. Though it seemed the serving dishes would go empty -- somehow, they refilled. And when we started to call the mamas by their names in the registry book, and they came forward to receive a mama kit from the pastors, the pile of kits didn't reduce. I personally witnessed it. I watched the pile for 40 minutes almost without blinking, and it didn't go down. We had 500 mama kits and 800 mamas, yet not a single woman went without – and? There were 118 mama kits leftover!"*

Our God is a miracle-working God. Nothing is too hard for Him. Nothing is impossible for God. He knows the needs, and He provides in abundance. God has no limits. His resources, power, strength, and might are inexhaustible. God continues to work and move today. Pray and watch what God will do!

Heavenly Father, thank You for the abundant care You give those who call to You. Thank You for the amazing, wonderful testimony of what You did for the mommas in Uganda. Open my eyes to watch You work, enlarge my vision and understanding of You so I may experience all You have to offer–exceedingly, abundantly more than I can ask or imagine. Help me never to limit You, or what You want to do, for everything is possible for You.

God's Timeless Truth

God "is able to [carry out His purpose and] do superabundantly more than all that we dare ask or think [infinitely beyond our greatest prayers, hopes, or dreams], according to His power that is at work within us" (Ephesians 3:20, AMP).
"For nothing is impossible with God" (Luke 1:37, NASB).

To read the original post, please visit The Lulu Tree -- https://thelulutree.com/blog/2018/04/16/the-miracle-of-the-mama-kits/

Pay the premiums

We have insurance for our car and house, along with life insurance. Each month, the premiums are due on our policies and must be paid.

If someone filled out forms promising to pay for insurance, if they told others they were buying insurance, would that be enough to purchase insurance?

If they wrote about their insurance, constantly visited the insurance office, if they spoke at conferences, traveled the country, even recruited others to buy that insurance, would that be enough?

If they did all those things and more, would that be enough? Or would they actually have to pay the premiums?

Wouldn't one actually have to pay for insurance to have a valid insurance policy?

Christianity is more than filling out a form, more than a casual statement, church-attendance, or being sprinkled at infancy.

Christianity is life-giving from the One who is Life. True Christianity, a true follower of Christ, is one who makes Jesus Lord of their life, and in return is given eternal life in the fullness of Jesus Christ.

Christianity isn't just a casual acquaintance, true Christianity is a life-long, moment-by-moment commitment to lay down your life to live for Christ, and in return you get to live in the fullness and joy of Jesus Christ.

Jesus said, "The sheep that are My own hear and are listening to My voice; and I know them, and they follow Me." And, "if you [really] love Me, you will keep (obey) My commands" (John 10:27, John 14:15, AMP).

Christianity is beyond action or head-knowledge, it is heart-deep, soul-deep commitment to follow Christ. In that beautiful commitment comes a relationship with The Prince of Peace who gives His fullness of joy and eternal life.

Jesus paid the premium sacrifice for our sins; all we must do is believe and follow. When Jesus lives in your heart, your life is changed from the inside out through the touch of His love. Please make sure you're committed, because being a Christian is one premium whose cost is worthy of everything.

Jesus, thank You for the sacrifice You made to give me freedom. I believe You are the Savior, the Son of God who takes away the sins of the world. I believe that God raised You from the dead. I believe in You, Jesus; I lay down my life to You, be the Lord of my life. Thank You for Your grace, mercy, and salvation!

God's Timeless Truth

God so loved the world that He gave His one and only Son, that whoever believes in Him shall not perish but have eternal life. God demonstrates His own love toward us, in that while we were yet sinners, Christ died for us (John 3:16, Romans 5:8).

Therefore, "If you acknowledge and confess with your mouth that Jesus is Lord [recognizing His power, authority, and majesty as God], and believe in your heart that God raised Him from the dead, you will be saved. For with the heart a person believes [in Christ as Savior] resulting in his justification [that is, being made righteous—being freed of the guilt of sin and made acceptable to God]; and with the mouth he acknowledges and confesses [his faith openly], resulting in and confirming [his] salvation. For the Scripture says, 'Whoever believes in Him [whoever adheres to, trusts in, and relies on Him] will not be disappointed [in his expectations]'" (Romans 10:9-11, AMP).

Little words

My head throbbed with pain. Several of my neck discs have collapsed and a muscle in my neck occasionally tightens, which causes a migraine-like sensation that feels like someone has jabbed a spike in the back of my head.

Tossing and turning during the night I hoped sleep would relax the muscles. By morning, my neck was feeling much better. However, when my husband asked how I was, I responded that I was doing a "little" better.

Little? I immediately felt a pain of guilt. I had minimized the truth. I asked the Lord for forgiveness and spoke truth to my husband that I was *much* better.

I wondered what if the words I said, came true? What if the words spoken, resulted in an action? What if my body heard the word "little" and decided to only have a little healing? Ack!

Our words contain life or death (Proverbs 18:21). Every word spoken results in an internal and external action. I sure don't want any little word to result in a big consequence. What if our words are what hinders us?

How many times have you heard ...?
I'm doing a little better.
I'm feeling a little better.
We are financially a little better.
The job is a little better.
The situation is a little better.
My health is a little better.
Things are just a little better.
The _____ is a little better.

Perhaps those words were true, but what if the words were spoken to minimize the situation, to gain sympathy, or because of doubt; and as a result, minimized what God is doing in our lives?

What if we took a moment before we spoke words, to make sure our words are completely true? What if we fully believed, trusted, and spoke words to make sure we are never hindered in our walk with the Lord or with others?

Let's live large in the truth by not allowing any little thing (in word or deed) to hinder our walk with God. Speak truth, for our every word, even our little words, have big consequences.

Heavenly Father, thank You for Your truth. Please help me to be very careful with my words, and even my thoughts, so that I never hinder You or minimize what You are doing in my life. Help me to always speak the truth, remembering that every word spoken comes with consequences. Help me, Father, to speak carefully so that I will always honor You and bring glory to Your name.

God's Timeless Truth

"...death and life are in the power of the tongue, and those who love it and indulge it will eat its fruit and bear the consequences of their words." (Proverbs 18:21, AMP).

"For by your words you will be justified, and by your words you will be condemned" (Matthew 12:37, NASB).

"Let the words of my mouth and the meditation of my heart be acceptable in Your sight, O Lord, my rock and my Redeemer" (Psalm 19:14, NASB).

Still jumping

Rubbing tired eyes, wiping sweat from dirty brows, the fishermen again hauled in empty nets. Even with years of experience and excellent skills, the men had fished all night and yet nothing showed for their hard work. Now on the shore, the three men washed their nets and hoped for a better day.

Then a man came, got in Simon's boat, and asked him to put out a little way from the land. The man, Jesus, began teaching as Simon listened.

After Jesus finished, He asked Simon to go to the deep water and let down his nets for a catch.

The fisherman responded, "Master, we worked hard all night and caught nothing, but I will do as You say and let down the nets."

When Simon let down his nets, fish that alluded him all night, now jumped into his nets. So many fish jumped in, that his friends came and filled their boats with so many fish their vessels began to sink (Luke 5:1-11).

When money was needed to pay a tax, Jesus told Peter to go to the sea and throw in a hook and take the first fish that comes up; and when you open its mouth, you will find a shekel. Take that and give it to them for you and Me" (Matthew 17:24-27). A need was met by a fish jumping on a hook.

Later, after Jesus was crucified and raised from the dead, He stood on the beach and called to His disciples, but they didn't know it was Jesus. "Children, you do not have any fish, do you?" He asked.

They answered Him, 'No.'

Jesus told them to cast the net on the right-hand side of the boat and they would find a catch. So, they cast, and then they were not able to haul it in because their nets were full of 153 large fish!

God's stories, God's miracles, don't end in the Bible or 2000 years ago; He continues to work in our day.

Only a few months ago, hunger growled at the stomachs of four young children. Although hungry, Pastor Manuel and his family made their way by canoe to church. Amazon floods had saturated crops and left them without food in the house and unable to fish in the swollen river.

After the service ended, another pastor asked Manuel if he would minister to a church down river. Planning on dropping off his very hungry wife and children at their home before serving the other congregation, they paddled toward their house.

Manuel assured his wife, ""The Lord will take care of us. I know it. We just need to be faithful." Being faithful on an empty stomach, and worried about your children going hungry isn't easy. They continued their journey in silence.

Then, with a mighty splash, an enormous, fish shot out of the water and landed in their boat. With screams of surprise and glee, they wrestled with a three-foot long, God-given fish. This wasn't just any fish; this arowana fish is a delicacy in the fish market that fed their family for a week.

God is a God of abundance, and when God tells fish to jump, they jump with joy to follow their Master's call.

Are you in need?

God, who created the heavens and earth, can do all things in heaven and earth. Nothing is impossible for God. Take your need to the One who made you, will take care of you, and loves you with an unfailing love. Whatever your need, remember God's miracles continue today and His provision comes in amazing, miraculous ways.

The fish are still jumping!

Heavenly Father, thank You for Your wonderful provision and Your amazing miracles. Thank You that even the fish jump for joy to do Your will. Please open my eyes to see how You provide and help me watch You work. And Father, help me to be like those fish and joyfully jump when You tell me to jump. Praise You, Father!

God's Timeless Truth

"And my God will supply all your needs according to His riches in glory in Christ Jesus" (Philippians 4:19, NASB).

To read the original Amazon story about Pastor Manuel, please visit Kelly Minter's website...
-- https://kellyminter.com/2018/04/12/a-big-fish-story-from-the-amazon/

Resume the journey

When the Israelites first came to the promised land, even though God had done mighty and marvelous things for their freedom, and even though God would continue to be with them as they took possession, they still didn't trust God. Therefore, the Israelites wandered for forty years because they were not obedient.

Except for Joshua and Caleb, the older generation perished, and never were able to take possession of what God had offered.

When the Israelites resumed their journey toward the promised land, the Jordan river flowed at flood stage which made the way impossible for the millions of people needing to cross.

God instructed the priests carrying the ark to step into the Jordan. When they did, the river opened, making a way on dry ground for the people to pass over.

Once they had crossed, "the priests carrying the ark of the Lord's covenant came up from the middle of the Jordan, and their feet stepped out on solid ground, the waters of the Jordan resumed their course, flowing over all the banks as before" (Joshua 1:8, HCSB).

The priests had to step in for the river to open, and they had to step out for the river to close. And from there, the Israelites had to enter to take possession of the promised land. Obedience requires putting 'faith-feet' in gear to step out in faith.

To get what God offers takes effort, trust, **and** action.

I wonder how often God has prompted me to obey and step out in faith, but I refused because of my own fears or insecurities?

I wonder how often I hindered the blessings God wanted to give me (and my family) because I refused to resume the journey and refused to take possession of what God offered. I don't want to miss what God is doing. I don't want to miss watching God work.

Let's not miss God's blessings. Let's not delay stepping out in faith, and let's not miss the opportunity to experience God's power.

When God tells us to resume the journey and go, let's move forward to take possession of what God offers.

Oh Father, thank You for Your guidance and the blessings You offer. Please forgive me. I am so sorry. I can think of many times something was offered by Your hand, and yet I declined because of my own thoughts and fears, my own view of what might happen, or what the cost would be for me or my family. I'm so sorry. Please forgive me. I'm so sorry, because the true cost of my not being obedient, broke Your heart, stopped Your blessings, hindered me moving forward and growing, and also hindered my family.

I'm so sorry. Please forgive me. Help me resume the journey and get moving when You tell me to go!

God's Timeless Truth

"If you [really] love Me, you will keep and obey My commandments" (John 14:15, AMP).
"Faith, if it does not have works (deeds and actions of obedience to back it up), by itself is destitute of power (inoperative, dead)" (James 2:17, AMPC).

Jesus said, "blessed are those who hear the word of God and keep it!" Luke 11:28, NKJV).

Therefore, let us "lay aside every encumbrance and the sin which so easily entangles us, and let us run with endurance the race that is set before us, fixing our eyes on Jesus..." (Hebrews 12:1-2, NASB).

Seed shooters

The witch-hazel tree bears yellow, ribbonlike flowers along with woody capsules containing seeds. During late fall or early winter, the tree's flowers curl in and the woody capsules dry. Hiking through the woods, you may be blessed to hear the very audible sound of the tree's seed capsules bursting open, propelling the seeds with force across the forest floor.

The visual reminds me of our life with Christ -- His love flowers in our hearts, opening our souls to His love, planting the seed of His forgiveness, grace, and mercy. His seed is given freely to us, to freely give to others, and as we explode with His love, His love scatters to the world.

"As for what was sown on good soil, this is the one who hears the word and understands it. He indeed bears fruit and yields, in one case a hundredfold, in another sixty, and in another thirty" (Matthew 13:23, ESV).

Has the love of Christ bloomed in your heart? If so, how can you spread the love of Christ?

Heavenly Father, thank You for the free gift You have given through the forgiveness, grace, and mercy of Jesus Christ. Help me to spread Your Good News everywhere I go.

God's Timeless Truth

"Jesus said to his followers, 'Go everywhere in the world, and tell the Good News to everyone.'" (Mark 16:15 NCV).

"This same Good News that came to you is going out all

over the world. It is bearing fruit everywhere by changing lives, just as it changed your lives from the day you first heard and understood the truth about God's wonderful grace" (Colossians 1:6, NLT).

May we be like Paul who wrote, "I do everything to spread the Good News and share in its blessings" (1 Corinthians 9:23, NLT).

Through the wound

A membrane formed on the back of my eye, puckering, and causing my vision to be distorted. The retina had torn, inflaming the optical nerve. Surgery was the only option for healing.

Fortunately, the operation went extremely well. Although I continue to have some distortion, time should continue the healing. Without that eye-wound being healed, my eyesight would continue to worsen and possibly lead to blindness.

We all have wounds. We've all been wounded. The devil wants those wounded to stay in their wounded state, to remain trapped in the pain. If we don't come to God with our wounds, if we refuse God's healing, we can't see beyond our wounded areas which leads to a distortion of our view of others, ourselves, and the world.

God is the Great Physician, Jehovah Rapha--the God who heals. Jesus came to bind the broken-hearted, heal wounds and heal lives. Nothing is impossible for God and nothing can stop the love of God.

We don't have to walk as the wounded. Jesus offers freedom, rest, and healing for every wound and every soul that comes to Him. The compassion, grace, and mercy of Jesus Christ restores sight blinded by sins committed against us and sins we have committed.

Jesus sets captives free and restores what the enemy meant for evil and makes all things new. Please don't allow the devil to keep you trapped in your wound. Come to the One wounded for you, who reaches out with nail-scarred hands to bring healing and restoration.

Jesus asks, "Do you want to get well? Come to Me and I will give you rest" (John 5:1-9, Matthew 11:28).

"When we press past the pain in prayer, when we press into Jesus, peace sutures bleeding hearts and holds them tenderly until they heal."
~ Gwen Smith[iv]

Heavenly Father, I come to You with my wounds. You know how deep the pain and how deep the hurt. Oh Father, please heal me. Thank You that You care. Thank You that You will give me a new day and a new start. Thank You that nothing is too hard for You. Thank You that Your mercies are new every morning. Thank You that You cause all things to work together for good for those who love You and are called according to Your purpose.

Help me see beyond my wounds to see what You are doing, how You are working, and how You are healing. I am Yours, Father. I place my wounds in Your tender hands for Your healing.

God's Timeless Truth

"Heal me, O Lord, and I will be healed; save me and I will be saved, for You are my praise" (Jeremiah 17:14, NASB).

"My soul, praise the Lord, and do not forget all His benefits. He forgives all your sin; He heals all your diseases. He redeems your life from the pit; He crowns you with faithful love and compassion" (Psalm 103:2-4, HCSB).

"Do not remember the past events, pay no attention to things of old. Look, I am about to do something new; even now it is coming. Do you not see it? Indeed, I will make a way in the wilderness, rivers in the desert" (Isaiah 43:18-19, HCSB).

"We know that all things work together for the good of those who love God: those who are called according to His purpose" (Romans 8:28, HCSB).

Prayer for the hurting

Heavenly Father, many are alone, many are hurting, many need Your tender touch. We bring our prayer before Your loving throne.

For those who are alone or have lost loved ones, please magnify Your presence, comfort, and peace.

For those whose finances are lacking, please multiply the loaves and fishes to meet each and every need.

For those who feel surrounded by the enemy, please open their eyes to see Your angelic army surrounding them.

For those who are groping in darkness, shine Your light of truth and mercy.

For those who are homeless, thank You they can dwell forever in Your presence and have a wonderful eternal home with You.

For those who are afraid, remind them of Your might, power, and complete authority.

For those who are in difficult situations, shelter them in the shadow of Your powerful wings.

Father, wrap them tenderly in Your love. Hold them close as You wipe every precious tear.

Bless them to feel You in a new, real, and vibrant way. Place in their hearts the joy of You.

Thank You Father that You are gentle with hurting hearts.

God's Timeless Truth

"Lord, you know the hopes of the helpless. Surely you will hear their cries and comfort them" (Psalm 10:17, NLT).

"Remember your promise to me; it is my only hope. Your promise revives me; it comforts me in all my troubles" (Psalm 119:49-50, NLT).

"When doubts filled my mind, your comfort gave me renewed hope and cheer" (Psalm 94:19, NLT).

"Even when I walk through the darkest valley, I will not be afraid, for you are close beside me. Your rod and your staff protect and comfort me" (Psalm 23:4, NLT).

"Now let your unfailing love comfort me, just as you promised me, your servant" (Psalm 119:76, NLT).

"God blesses those who mourn, for they will be comforted." (Matthew 5:4, NLT).

"The Lord is close to the brokenhearted; he rescues those whose spirits are crushed" (Psalm 34:18, NLT).

"He heals the brokenhearted and bandages their wounds" (Psalm 147:3, NLT).

"Father to the fatherless, defender of widows—this is God, whose dwelling is holy" (Psalm 68:5, NLT).

"For the Lamb on the throne will be their Shepherd. He will lead them to springs of life-giving water. And God will wipe every tear from their eyes" (Revelation 7:17, NLT).

May I see your identification?

We all have an identity. Our passport or driver's license contains basic information, yet inside each of us we carry an identity, a label someone gave us, or we gave ourselves. I know many people who carry the wrong identification; they use their past failures, or the bad things that happened to them for their identity.

I have good news. You are **not** your failure, your sin(s), your loss, your divorce, your abortion, your victimhood, your illness, your family heritage, your job title, your difficulty or struggle. What happens may hurt and wound, but don't allow anyone (including yourself) to define you by what happened in the past. The only valid identification is who you are in Christ. As a Christian, when God looks at you, He sees His beloved, sinless Son shining through your heart.

When we have given our lives to Christ, we are secure in Christ. Our identity is a child of the King of kings and Lord of lords. Even if a bad thing or failure happened after you were a Christian, your identity remains a beloved child of the Creator of the universe.

In Christ, you are given the power **daily** to heal, move forward, be restored, mended, remade, and recreated. Moment by moment God's compassion, lovingkindness, and mercies pour forth on His children.

Moment by moment God gives grace and equips you to walk through whatever you have walked through, and whatever you are walking through, and whatever will come next.

When Christ is in your heart, you are plugged into our All-powerful, ALL-mighty God.

No matter what may come against you, God's unfailing love is already there to help, fight for you, equip you, restore you, and give you everything needed for every need.

Now, when you think of your identification, always remember your true identity is in Jesus Christ.

God, thank You that through Your Son, Jesus Christ, I have an everlasting identity as Your beloved child. Thank You that I am forgiven, renewed, and restored through Your grace. Thank You that I am a new creation in You!

God's Timeless Truth

"I have been crucified with Christ and I no longer live, but Christ lives in me. The life I now live in the body, I live by faith in the Son of God, who loved me and gave himself for me. If anyone is in Christ, he is a new creature; the old things passed away; behold, new things have come" (Galatians 2:20, NIV), (2 Corinthians 5:17, NASB).

Streams

Troubled by concerns for a loved one, I left a message with a friend asking if she would join in prayer. Within minutes she called to bring encouragement, support, and prayer. During her prayer, she mentioned as believers we aren't just given a stream of living water, we are given streams of living water. Oh, my. I knew this, but her prayer caused streams to bubble up with renewed truth.

One of my favorite things is to sit by a river or stream and spend time with God. When I think of the verses in Psalm 1:1-3, I picture myself happily planted by a stream.

The wonderful truth is God blesses with more than one stream. He says those who delight in God and meditate on His word will be like a tree planted firm by streams of water. And Jesus promises that those who believe in Him will have rivers of living water flowing from within them.

Oh, how this thrills my soul. The influx of God's life-giving water comes through Jesus Christ streaming into our souls, planting us in the streams of His living water, so that our souls gush out with springs and rivers of living water.

God's 'living water grace' washes away sins. His 'living water love' is for your lonely, hurting heart. He supplies 'living water help' for your every need and every decision.

His 'living water intercession' is for your every prayer, and 'His living water mercies' are new every morning.

God's living water protects, restores, and renews, and is available for every day of your life. God gives living water to stand firm in a world shaken by the enemy, comforting all your pain, and courage for every discouragement.

His living water, Red Sea dividing, water walking, storm-stilling power never leaves you powerless.

God's living water streams toward you, in you, and through you. His soul-giving, life-living water flows, gushes, and forever streams with rivers from our generous, loving God.

Dive deep in the grace of Jesus Christ, allow His living water to pour into you, and splash onto those around you.

Heavenly Father, I'm rejoicing in the truth of Your amazing, life-giving, living water. Jesus, thank You for the streams of living water that comes from You. Heavenly Father, thank You for the promises You have given in Your word. Thank You that You are always doing new things. Thank You that You promise to pour out Your Spirit on our thirsty, dry souls where You make streams in the desert.

Thank You, Father. May I rejoice always in the blessings of Your living water, eternal grace. Pour Your living water within me so that Your living water will flow to others.

God's Timeless Truth

"He who believes in Me [who cleaves to and trusts in and relies on Me] as the Scripture has said, from his innermost being shall flow [continuously] springs and rivers of living water" (John 7:38, AMPC).

"How blessed is the man who does not walk in the counsel of the wicked, nor stand in the path of sinners, nor sit in the seat of scoffers! But his delight is in the law of the Lord, and in His law, he meditates day and night. He will be like a tree firmly planted by streams of water, which yields its fruit in its season and its leaf does not wither; and in whatever he does, he prospers" (Psalm 1:1-3, NASB).

"I will pour out water on the thirsty land and streams on the dry ground; I will pour out My Spirit on your offspring and My blessing on your descendants; and they will spring up among the grass like poplars by streams of water" (Isaiah 44:3-4, NASB).

"See, I am doing a new thing! Now it springs up; do you not perceive it? I am making a way in the wilderness and streams in the wasteland" (Isaiah 43:19, NIV).

"There is a river whose streams make glad the city of God, the holy dwelling places of the Most High" (Psalm 46:4, NASB).

Bring them to Jesus

Remember to pray, remember to bring your children, your loved ones, your friends, the lost, bring them all to Jesus in prayer. For the prayer of a righteous man is powerful and effective.

Bring your children to Jesus. Synagogue officials, Jews, Gentiles, Centurions, mothers, fathers, brought their children to Jesus. Whether they came with large faith or small faith, every need was met by the love and compassion of Christ Jesus (Matthew 9:18-25, Matthew 15:21-28, Matthew 8:5-13, Mark 9:17-27, Matthew 19:13-14).

When Jesus walked this earth, large crowds came to Him, bringing those who were lame, crippled, blind, mute, and laid them at His feet; and He healed them. They brought all who were ill, suffering with various diseases and pains, demoniacs, epileptics, paralytics; and He healed them (Matthew 15:30, Matthew 4:24).

The blind, lame, leper, hemorrhaging, demon-possessed, the curious, and the prodigal are all met by the love, forgiveness, and healing of Christ Jesus and our merciful Heavenly Father (Matthew 9:20-22, Matthew 20:30-34, Luke 19:10, Luke 15:11-32, Matthew 8:1-3, Luke 17:11-16, Luke 8:1-3).

Four men came with their paralytic friend to Jesus. Unable to reach Him because of the crowds, they removed the roof above Jesus, dug an opening, then let down the pallet on which their friend laid and Jesus healed him (Mark 2:1-12).

Bring your family to Jesus and bring your friends to Jesus. Carry them through prayer, tear through the roof of heaven and bring them to Jesus.

Christ Jesus is the healer, restorer, redeemer, the One who died to set us free. Bring yourself and bring others to Jesus. No need is too small, no need too great, no sin too dark, no wound too deep for Christ Jesus. Bring yourself, bring them, bring them all to Jesus.

Jesus, thank You that You are my Savior. Thank You that You are a healing, restoring, redeeming Savior. Thank You that I can come to You and bring my needs and the needs of others to You. Thank You that You care and You hear when I call to You.

Savior, please save me, save my loved ones, and move in the heart of those who are lost that they will come to You.

God's Timeless Truth

Christ Jesus is ...at the right hand of God, interceding for us. Jesus... continues forever, holds His priesthood permanently. Therefore, He is able also to save forever those who draw near to God through Him, since He always lives to make intercession for them (Romans 8:34, Hebrews 7:24-25, NASB).

Bring the lost to Jesus in prayer. "As I live! declares the Lord God, I take no pleasure in the death of the wicked, but rather that the wicked turn from his way and live. Turn back, turn back from your evil ways! Therefore, repent and return, so that your sins may be wiped away, in order that times of refreshing may come from the presence of the Lord. I tell you, there is joy in the presence of the angels of God over one sinner who repents" (Ezekiel 33:11, NASB, Acts 3:19,

NASB, Luke 15:10, NASB). This is the confidence which we have before Him, that, if we ask anything according to His will, He hears us. And if we know that He hears us in whatever we ask, we know that we have the requests which we have asked from Him. The effective prayer of a righteous man can accomplish much. Elijah was a man with a nature like ours, and he prayed earnestly that it would not rain, and it did not rain on the earth for three years and six months (1 John 5:14-15, James 5:16-17, NASB). Pray and bring your need to Jesus.

Prayer for the lost ones...

"Hear my prayer, O God; give ear to the words of my mouth (Psalm 54:2). Heavenly Father, You are the God who sees (Genesis 16:13). You are the God who hears (Psalm 4:3). You are the God who is faithful to the generations of the righteous (Psalm 100:5). Oh, God I ask for Your mercy and kindness to be poured out on our children, their children, our families, and beyond (Psalm 112:1-2).

God, please open the eyes of the ones who have run from You. Open the eyes of the wayward that they will find You, for You are The Way. Open their ears to hear You.

Father, I pray Your spirit of wisdom, revelation, and knowledge may be poured out on them. I pray that the eyes of their heart may be enlightened so that they will know the hope of Your calling and the riches of the glory of Your inheritance, and the surpassing greatness of Your power toward those who believe (Ephesians 1:17-19).

Jesus, You are the Son of Man who came to seek and save that which was lost (Luke 19:10). Save them, Lord.

God, You search for the lost sheep and joyfully bring them home. You search for that which was lost and rejoice when found. Oh Father, joyfully bring home my lost loved one (Luke 15:3-9).

Thank You, Lord, that You hear my voice and my cry (Psalm 116:1), Psalm 34:17). Thank You that nothing is impossible for You! (Luke 1:37).

Thank You that one day we will rejoice along with the angels when our loved ones come home (Luke 15:10).

I ask these things in the name of Jesus Christ, who is my Savior. Amen.

Loving enough

She pulled me aside, whispered in my ear saying my conduct at that moment was not the best. At the time, I didn't want to hear what my friend said, and sadly I didn't take her advice. Because I didn't listen, that one messy moment became an even bigger mess.

I never thanked her all those years ago, but I am grateful my friend loved me enough to tell me what I was doing was wrong.

I want to be like my friend. I want to be loving enough, compassionate enough, caring enough, to speak the truth. I'm truly not loving if I tell someone they can ignore their sin, or live in their sin, because sin breaks God's heart and blocks relationship and communion with a Holy God.

God longs to bring us into His presence, loving so much that He sent His only Son to earth to be a sacrifice for our sins, to bridge the gap with His love so that we could come into His loving presence.

Jesus blesses us with an example. A shamed woman, caught in the very act of adultery, was flung at the feet of Jesus.

Angry men taunted and begged for the opportunity to stone her. But Jesus replied, "He who is without sin among you, let him be the first to throw a stone."

When they heard it, they began to depart one by one, beginning with the older ones.

Jesus left alone with the woman in the center of the court, straightened up and said to her, "'Woman, where are they? Did no one condemn you?'

She said, 'No one, Lord.'

And Jesus said, 'I do not condemn you, either. Go. From now on sin no more'" (John 8:1-11). Jesus, the sinless one, offered grace to the sinner, loving her enough to tell her to sin no more.

I want to be like Jesus -- loving enough to speak the truth in love, because God's truth sets people free (John 8:32).

Heavenly Father, thank You for Your forgiveness, mercy, and grace. Help me not ignore sin. Help me to run from sin and run to You. Help me to be loving enough to address sin and point others to Your wonderful, loving grace and mercy. Help me to be like Charles Spurgeon and tell others of Your wonderful love.

> *"Fling wide, then, the portals of your soul. He will come with that love which you long to feel; he will come with that joy into which you cannot work your poor depressed spirit; he will bring the peace which now you have not. ... Only open the door to him, drive out his enemies, give him the keys of your heart, and he will dwell there forever. Oh, wondrous love, that brings such a guest to dwell in such a heart! ...The whole of Christ, in His adorable character as the Son of God, is by Himself made over to us most richly to enjoy. His wisdom is our direction, his knowledge our instruction, his power our protection, his justice our surety, his love our comfort, his mercy our solace, and his immutability our trust. He makes no reserve but*

opens the recesses of the Mount of God and bids us dig in its mines for the hidden treasures."
~ Charles Spurgeon

God's Timeless Truth

"For God did not send the Son into the world to judge the world, but that the world might be saved through Him" (John 3:17).

"For the wages of sin is death, but the free gift of God [that is, His remarkable, overwhelming gift of grace to believers] is eternal life in Christ Jesus our Lord. Therefore, there is now no condemnation [no guilty verdict, no punishment] for those who are in Christ Jesus [who believe in Him as personal Lord and Savior]. For the law of the Spirit of life [which is] in Christ Jesus [the law of our new being] has set you free from the law of sin and of death" (Romans 6:23, Romans 8:1-2, AMP).

He knows how you feel

One of the beautiful blessings of Christianity is when we ask Jesus into our hearts, He lives in our hearts (John 15). Through Jesus, we are given a wonderful blessing of an intimate relationship with our Savior and with our Heavenly Father.

As I pondered this today, I realized whatever I'm feeling (and facing), Jesus understands.

Jesus understands what we are going through because He walked this earth and knows the pains and trials of humanity.

God made us, formed us, then loved us enough to send His Son to live among us and then within us. Jesus intimately understands our emotions because He is intimately living within us.

So, when you are lonely, He knows how you feel because He is there within you.

When you are hurt, He knows how you feel. Jesus's sympathy goes beyond head knowledge; He has heart knowledge because His tender heart beats within your tender heart.

Jesus truly knows how you feel. Whatever you are feeling, whatever you are facing, you are not alone. Jesus is with you and He truly knows how you feel.

Jesus, thank You that You live within me. Thank You that You truly know how I feel. You know the number of hairs on my head and the thoughts I think in my head. You know every word I say before I even say them.

You know my desires, my needs, everything about me,

and You still love me. Thank You!

Jesus, thank You for loving me enough to live in my heart. Please take my heart, make it fully Yours, and fill my heart with You. Thank You that You made me and You know me. Thank You that You think about me, have good plans for me, and You always truly know how I feel.

God's Timeless Truth

"For we do not have a high priest who cannot sympathize with our weaknesses, but One who has been tempted in all things as we are, yet without sin" (Hebrews 4:15, NASB).

God, "You know when I sit down and when I get up. You know my thoughts before I think them. You know where I go and where I lie down. You know everything I do. Lord, even before I say a word, You already know it" (Psalm 139:2-4, NCV).

"Oh yes, you shaped me first inside, then out; you formed me in my mother's womb. I thank you, High God—you're breathtaking! Body and soul, I am marvelously made! I worship in adoration—what a creation! You know me inside and out, you know every bone in my body; you know exactly how I was made, bit by bit, how I was sculpted from nothing into something. Like an open book, you watched me grow from conception to birth; all the stages of my life were spread out before you, the days of my life all prepared before I'd even lived one day. Your thoughts—how rare, how beautiful! God, I'll never comprehend them! I couldn't even begin to count them—any more than I could count the sand of the sea" (Psalm 139:15-18, MSG).

Who is God?

He is love.
He is just.
He is pure.
He is hope.
He is truth.
He is great.
He is good.
He is Holy.
He is peace.
He is eternal.
He is patient.
He is exalted.
He is a guide.
He is a shield.
He is freedom.
He is flawless.
He is majestic.
He is merciful.
He is gracious.
He is forgiving.
He is powerful.
He is righteous.
He is your rock.
He is blameless.
He is ever lasting.
He is your refuge.
He is your Savior.
He is your rescuer.
He delights in you.

He is your teacher.
He is your support.
He is your strength.
He lights your way.
He is slow to anger.
He goes before you.
He is your deliverer.
He is your protector.
He directs your path.
He is your Shepherd.
He is compassionate.
He is your comforter.
He watches over you.
He directs your steps.
He restores your soul.
He saves the afflicted.
He is your stronghold.
He is a consuming fire.
He takes delight in you.
He rewards the faithful.
He hears when you call.
He will never leave you.
He is abounding in love.
His love endures forever.
He is your strong fortress.
He will never forsake you.
He is the God who avenges.
He is a tower of deliverance.
He drives back your enemies.
He is a refuge for the oppressed.
He is close to the brokenhearted.

With God all things are possible.
He is a refuge in times of trouble.
He rejoices over you with singing.
He longs to show you compassion.
He loves you with an unfailing love.
He is light and in Him is no darkness.
He knows your weakness and helps you.
He saves those who are crushed in spirit.
He hides you in the shadow of His wings.
He guides you in the path of righteousness.
He is near to all who call upon Him in truth.
He shows His loving-kindness to His anointed.
He engraves your name on the palm of His hand.
God is love.

God is preparing a place in Heaven just for you, where there will be no more crying, no more death, pain, or mourning, where you will be safe forever in His love.

Dear God, thank You for who You are and all You are. Thank You for Your amazing, wonderful love!

God's Timeless Truth

Let the godly sing for joy to the Lord; it is fitting for the pure to praise Him. For the word of the Lord holds true, and we can trust everything He does. He loves whatever is just and good; the unfailing love of the Lord fills the earth. The Lord's plans stand firm forever; His intentions can never be shaken.

The Lord looks down from heaven and sees the whole

human race. From His throne He observes all who live on the earth. He made their hearts, so He understands everything they do. The Lord watches over those who fear Him, those who rely on His unfailing love. He rescues them from death and keeps them alive in times of famine. We put our hope in the Lord. He is our help and our shield. In Him our hearts rejoice, for we trust in His holy name. Let Your unfailing love surround us, Lord, for our hope is in You alone. There is no one like You, Lord, and there is no God but You. Taste and see that the Lord is good. Oh, the joys of those who take refuge in Him (Psalm 33:1, Psalm 33:4-5, Psalm 33:11, Psalm 33:13-15, Psalm 33:18-22, 1 Chronicles 17:20, Psalm 34:8).

Known by love

Mother Teresa, admired by Christians and non-Christians, was known for her love. Her love showed and glowed through her actions and through her love for Jesus.

Loving comes with risks, and at times the heart will beat raw and sore, but loving deep is worth the effort. Profound love given, blesses in profound ways. We can hide our hearts away, lock it behind a stone fortress of self-protection, but self-protection only brings lonely fear. Mother Teresa loved with the love of Jesus. She knew the secret that when you love with Christ's love, love never runs out.

Oh, may we also love with the love of Jesus. The world is hurting, afraid, hopeless, and angry; they need to know there is hope, justice, comfort, strength, and grace found in the love of Christ. Jesus told us to go and tell and make disciples.

The world needs to know about Jesus. People need to know of The One who quiets the storms, who can do all things, who loves with an unfailing love, who promises to wipe away every tear, who will never leave, who takes what the enemy meant for evil and will turn it into good. They need to know this amazing love.

Please tell them. Tell them about Jesus.

Tell them what Jesus has done for you. They need to know someone made it to the other side of grief, confusion, sadness, job loss, cancer, medical issues, family issues, heartache, and pain.... People need to know they also can make it through.

That's why I write. That's why I share some of the things I never wanted to share.

I want people to know they too can make it through, for they too have a Savior who loves them even with their mess and sin and deep needs.

They need to know and you can help. You can point to our loving Savior.

They need to know Who you know. Because God will help you through and help them through. They need to know. Please tell them Who you know and "...tell them what great things the Lord has done for you, and how He has had compassion on you" (Mark 5:19, NKJV).

Love with the love of Christ. Love one another, loving with the gentle, tenderhearted, kindness, and patience of our Heavenly Father. May we be known by the love of our loving God.

Heavenly Father, thank You for Your unfailing love. Oh, how I want the world to know You and Your amazing love. Thank You for the wonderful ways You love us. Help me to freely share what You have done in my life and freely share Your love with others. Help me to be known by Your love so that I can share Your love.

God's Timeless Truth

"Jesus came and told his disciples, 'I have been given all authority in heaven and on earth. Therefore, go and make disciples of all the nations, baptizing them in the name of the Father and the Son and the Holy Spirit. Teach these new disciples to obey all the commands I have given you. And be sure of this: I am with you always, even to the end of the age'" (Matthew 28:18-20, NLT).

"This is how God showed his love to us: He sent his one and only Son into the world so that we could have life through him. This is what real love is: It is not our love for God; it is God's love for us. He sent his Son to die in our place to take away our sins. Dear friends, if God loved us that much, we also should love each other" (1 John 4:9-11, NCV).

Jesus said, "love one another, even as I have loved you, that you also love one another. By this all men will know that you are My disciples, if you have love for one another" (John 13:34-35, NASB).

"Let everything you do be done in love [motivated and inspired by God's love for us]" (1 Corinthians 16:14, AMP).

See the good

The world is a dark place. People are angry, ranting, and raving, disgusted with one another, and disgusted with life. Sometimes it's hard to see the good.

Fortunately, we do have a choice. We have a choice what we watch, what we read, and what we allow our minds to dwell upon. We have a choice how we live and what we choose to see.

Good things **are** happening. Look to Christ, read His word, remember our good God is always in control. Never give up because God will never give up on you. God will never fail you, for His love is unfailing.

The Lord is good and His lovingkindness is everlasting (Psalm 136:1). Focus on Jesus, remember He is always good, fix your thoughts and your mind on His goodness.

Live in a way that others will see the good of Christ within you Shine as a bright light, a beacon of hope in this dark world. Live so the light of Christ shines bright with His joy, love, and peace.

Show the good of Christ to a world so needing the good glory of Christ.

May those who see the good of Jesus within us excitedly say, "we wish to see Jesus" (John 12:21).

Heavenly Father, thank You that You are good. Please open my eyes to see wonderful things in Your word (Psalm 119:18). Help me to see the good in You, to live in the good of You, so that others are drawn to Your wonderful goodness.

God's Timeless Truth

"How beautiful and delightful on the mountains are the feet of him who brings good news, who announces peace, who brings good news of good [things], who announces salvation, who says to Zion, 'Your God reigns!'" (Isaiah 52:7, AMP).

"Shine like stars in the world. Let your light shine before men in such a way that they may see your good works and glorify your Father who is in heaven" (Philippians 2:15, Matthew 5:16, NASB).

"Finally, believers, whatever is true, whatever is honorable and worthy of respect, whatever is right and confirmed by God's word, whatever is pure and wholesome, whatever is lovely and brings peace, whatever is admirable and of good repute; if there is any excellence, if there is anything worthy of praise, think continually on these things [center your mind on them, and implant them in your heart]" (Philippians 4:8, AMP).

In the shadow valleys

I had an interesting visual. A mass of people with angry faces fought and argued. Without fear or anxiety, I walked between them along an open pathway, my appearance merely a shadow as I moved unhindered and free through the crowds.

In the midst of our divisive world with people fighting and arguing, I realized God has given a choice, an opportunity, to walk free. Anger, division, and trials will come. One look at the news, or a few minutes on social media, and the world seems to be a powder keg waiting to explode.

However, we are given a beautiful truth in the book of Isaiah. "**You will guard him and keep him in perfect and constant peace whose mind [both its inclination and its character] is stayed on You, because he commits himself to You, leans on You, and hopes confidently in You.** So, trust in the Lord (commit yourself to Him, lean on Him, hope confidently in Him) forever; for the Lord God is an everlasting Rock [the Rock of Ages]" (Isaiah 26:3-4, AMPC). Emphasis added on scripture.

If we commit our mind, leaning on and hoping confidently in God, we are given His perfect and constant peace.

During the earthly ministry of Jesus, He encountered much opposition. "Then they took up stones to throw at Him; but Jesus hid Himself and went out of the temple, going through the midst of them, and so passed by" (John 8:59, NKJV). Jesus, concealed and hidden, passed through the midst of them.

We too are given the protection and concealment of God. The Psalms reminds us of God's great goodness which He stores up for those who fear Him, for those who take refuge in Him. He hides them in the secret place of His presence, sheltered in the shadow of His wings. Even when we walk through the valley of the shadow of death, He will be with us, and in the shadow of His wings we can sing for joy.

Psalm 91 reminds us that when we dwell in the secret place of the Most High, we abide in the shadow of the Almighty. He will cover us with His feathers and under His wings we will take refuge.

As we run to God, dwell in His presence, and focus our minds on Him, we can rest confidently in His everlasting lovingkindness and hope, nestled in the shelter and shadow of God's wings.

No matter how dark the day or night, you can walk free in the shadow valleys of our wonderful God.

Heavenly Father, thank You for Your goodness and love. Thank You that You are with me in the shadows. Thank You that I can run to You and hide under the shelter of Your wings. Thank You that You are a hiding place, a strong tower, comfort, and a refuge. Guide me, help me, and protect me in the loving shadow of Your wings.

God's Timeless Truth

"How great is Your goodness, which You have stored up for those who fear You, which You have wrought for those who take refuge in You, before the sons of men! You hide them in the secret place of Your presence from the conspiracies of man; You keep them secretly in a shelter from the strife of tongues. How precious is Your lovingkindness, O God! And the children of men take refuge in the shadow of Your wings. Even though I walk through the valley of the shadow of death, I fear no evil, for You are with me; Your rod and Your staff, they comfort me. For You have been my help, and in the shadow of Your wings I sing for joy" (Psalm 31:19-20, Psalm 36:7, Psalm 23:4, Psalm 63:7, NASB).

"He who dwells in the secret place of the Most High shall abide under the shadow of the Almighty. I will say of the Lord, 'He is my refuge and my fortress; my God, in Him I will trust.' Surely, He shall deliver you from the snare of the fowler and from the perilous pestilence. He shall cover you with His feathers, and under His wings you shall take refuge; His truth shall be your shield and buckler. You shall not be afraid of the terror by night, nor of the arrow that flies by day, nor of the pestilence that walks in darkness, nor of the destruction that lays waste at noonday. A thousand may fall at your side, and ten thousand at your right hand; but it shall not come near you. Only with your eyes shall you look, and see the reward of the wicked. Because you have made the Lord, who is my refuge, even the Most High, your dwelling place, no evil shall befall you, nor shall any plague come near your dwelling; for He shall give His angels charge over you, to keep you in all your ways. In their hands they shall bear you up, lest you dash your foot against a stone. You shall tread upon the lion and the cobra, the young lion and the serpent you shall trample underfoot. 'Because he has set his love upon Me, therefore I will deliver him; I will set him on high, because he has known My name. He shall call upon Me, and I will answer him; I will be with him in trouble; I will deliver him and honor him. With long life I will satisfy him, and show him My salvation" (Psalm 91, NKJV).

Would you pray for them?

During an intense time of prayer for a loved one, I felt the Holy Spirit whisper in my soul, "Would you pray as diligently for them as you pray for the ones you love?" The question rocked me because I knew He was referring to my prayers for those I am not as fond of, those I disagree with, those who impact my life in a negative way. It's easy to pray for those I love, not so easy to pray for others.

To be honest, I've found my prayers for my loved ones take on an intensity, fervor, and love I wasn't applying to my prayers for others. I need to do better. I need to be aware of my prayers and pray with the love of God for everyone. Pray with passion and pray with genuine concern for lost souls and those who have lost their way.

So, I'm asking these questions for us all...

Would you pray for others in the same way you pray for your loved one?

The lost person in your neighborhood, your apartment building, at your work, the one far away in the world. Would you pray for them?

The person who drove too slowly, the person who drives too fast, the one who cut you off in traffic. Would you pray for them?

The politician you don't like, the one who votes against your political party. Would you pray for them?

The bully, the boss that makes your life miserable, the neighbor that makes you want to move, the gang member. Would you pray for them?

Would you pray for the terrorist, the one who plots to kill? Would you pray for them?

Would you pray for your enemy, the one who hurt you the most? Would you pray for them?

The person you don't like, the politician you can't stand... what if you prayed for them? What if your prayer, your plea, would lead them to change, to become a Christ follower, to grow in Christ, and be a blessing to the world?

James reminds us, "The heartfelt and persistent prayer of a righteous man (believer) can accomplish much [when put into action and made effective by God—it is dynamic and can have tremendous power]" (James 5:16, AMP).

Pray, ask God, pray for God's perfect will. "...You do not have because you do not ask. You ask and do not receive, because you ask with wrong motives..." (James 4:2-3).

Instead of complaining, worrying, being angry and upset, please pray. Pray for God to move, to bless, to bring them into His presence and for their salvation.

Please pray for them.

Heavenly Father, thank You that I can come to You. Thank You that I can lift up my prayer to You. Father, it's hard sometimes to pray for the people I don't like or those I don't agree with, but You are a loving God and wish all to come to You and salvation through Your Son, Jesus Christ. Thank You that You know best. Thank You that You loved me before I loved You.

God, I lift up the person You have brought to mind. Help me to treat others the way I want others to treat me. Help me to love with Your love. Help me to trust You for You know best. You are good and do good. Help me not hinder You from working in their life.

Bless _____ with a heart to seek You and turn to You. Bless them to know You as Lord and Savior. Bless them Lord in the way You long to bless them.

Thank You that I can trust Your plans, for Your plans are always best. Help me to pray in a way that honors You. Thank You when I pray for others, truly pray for them, You give me peace, comfort, and bless me with a closer walk with You. Thank You, Father!

God's Timeless Truth

My heart's desire and my prayer to God for them is for their salvation (Romans 10:1).

Love your enemies, do good to those who hate you, bless those who curse you, pray for those who mistreat you. Treat others the same way you want them to treat you. I say to you, love your enemies and pray for those who persecute you, so that you may be sons of your Father who is in heaven (Luke 6:27-31, Matthew 5:44-45).

Elijah was a man with a nature like ours, and he prayed earnestly that it would not rain, and it did not rain on the earth for three years and six months. Therefore, pray without ceasing. Devote yourselves to prayer, keeping alert in it with an attitude of thanksgiving (James 5:17, 1 Thessalonians 5:17, Colossians 4:2).

For the heartfelt and persistent prayer of a righteous man (believer) can accomplish much when put into action and made effective by God—it is dynamic and can have tremendous power. And all things you ask in prayer, believing, you will receive (James 5:16, Matthew 21:22).

Crossing Jordan

The Israelites stood on the banks of the swollen Jordan river. The land promised by God stretched before them, a good land, flowing with abundance and new beginnings. Forty years earlier, the Israelites had been invited by God to take the land filled with a bounty of goodness. Yet, the Israelites had only seen the obstacles and focused on the people bigger than they and forgot their all-powerful God. They had forgotten God said He would go with them and help them. Their fear outweighed their faith. After forty years of wandering and waiting, they once again were invited to take possession of the land.

"Go through the camp and tell the people, 'Get your supplies ready. Three days from now you will cross the Jordan here to go in and take possession of the land the LORD your God is giving you for your own'" (Joshua 1:11, NIV).

For three days the people prepared and reflected on God's promises. The flooded Jordan river blocked their way, but the only thing that would keep them from the promised land would be their unbelief.

God instructed the priests to stand in the Jordan river. Nothing changed and nothing happened until the priests believed in God's promises and moved forward. Only when their feet touched the water, did the way become passable.

Faith calls for action.

When Noah was told to build the ark, I wonder how he built for decades without giving up hope, without stopping, while probably being taunted and criticized. Noah did not falter in his calling, he acted and he believed.

When Abraham was told to believe he would be the father of nations, he did not waver. Even though he was past the age to be a father, and Sarah was barren, Abraham had faith in God and the abilities of God -- Abraham believed.

Belief or unbelief is personal.

> *"God can do anything that's on His heart through the one who believes. The key is belief."*
> *~ Henry & Richard Blackaby, Claude King[v]*

Noah and Abraham did not deter from their belief in God and His ways. We too have a choice to believe and follow God. Fortunately, God is the One who qualifies and He is the One who equips. Yet, until we step into the Jordan, until our faith takes action, the waters will not move, arks don't get built, the promised child won't come, the promised land won't be given, and we will not see the amazing things that only come from believing God.

Are you standing on the edge of your Jordan? Do you see the water at flood stage or do you see your promised land?

Are you chained to the shoreline by unbelief? Can you look beyond the roaring waters and step in faith? Don't wait to move forward. If God has told you to cross... believe Him and cross.

> *"God does not ask you to give the perfect surrender in your strength, or by the power of your will; God is willing to work it in you. Do we not read: 'It is God that worketh in us, both to will and to do of his good pleasure' (Phil. 2:13)?*

> *And that is what we should seek for—to go on our faces before God, until our hearts learn to believe that the everlasting God Himself will come in to turn out what is wrong, to conquer what is evil, and to work what is well-pleasing in His blessed sight. God Himself will work it in you." ~ Andrew Murray[vi]*

Your power is not needed to get beyond the obstacles, to claim the promises, to step out in faith -- believing God results in the power of God. The power of God that created the heavens and earth, also creates, recreates, and makes all things new.

Believe God, believe in His All-powerful, mighty power. If God is telling you to go forward; step out in faith... all you must do is believe.

"Jesus looked at them and said, 'With man this is impossible, but not with God; all things are possible with God'" (Mark 10:27, NIV).

> *God "is not wanting great men, but He is wanting men who will dare to prove the greatness of their God." ~ A. B. Simpson*

Heavenly Father, I'm stepping out in faith. Thank You that You will supply the power needed and equip me for everything You have called me to accomplish. Lord, I believe; help my unbelief. Let me step out even when I can't see the step. Help me to trust that You will guide and lead me even when I can't see where You are leading. May I be like those listed in Hebrews who stepped out in faith. Father,

I want to cross over to follow You, for You have planned amazing things.

God's Timeless Truth

"By faith Abraham, when he was called, obeyed by going out to a place which he was to receive for an inheritance; and he went out, not knowing where he was going" (Hebrews 11:8, NASB).

"Noah did all that the Lord commanded him. By faith Noah, when warned about things not yet seen, in holy fear built an ark to save his family. By his faith he condemned the world and became heir of the righteousness that comes by faith" (Genesis 7:5, Hebrews 11:7, NASB).

"Teach me to do Your will, for You are my God; let Your good Spirit lead me on level ground" (Psalm 143:10, NASB).

"He restores my soul; He guides me in the paths of righteousness for His name's sake (Psalm 23:3, NASB).

"For You are my rock and my fortress; for Your name's sake You will lead me and guide me" (Psalm 31:3, NASB).

"With Your counsel You will guide me, and afterward receive me to glory" (Psalm 73:24, NASB).

Fired up

Years ago, I lived in the Smoky mountains in a small town near the border of North Carolina. In winter, many people burned coal to keep warm. I did not realize the heat, power, and longevity of that little black rock until I placed a small lump in my fireplace.

Coal is only a rock, but when ignited, glows, warms, and creates a super-hot, long-lasting fire. Coal is used for refining metals. Coal under pressure becomes a diamond. Who knew what power could be released in a little rock?

Jesus is The Rock, The Cornerstone. We're just little rocks until our world is rocked by The Rock. When Jesus' love fires within us, our sins are consumed by His grace and mercy. His light, His Holy Fire refines, cleanses, and shines eternal light.

Our God in His gracious mercy is the consuming fire that burns away our sin (Malachi 3:3). The refiner's fire tests, examines, displaying the nature of the object tested. God is the consuming fire that burns away the temporal to give us the eternal (Zechariah 13:9). His Holy flame burns away things that block His peace, His joy, His love, and His glory (Psalm 66:10).

The fiery testing proves genuine faith, for a faith that works in the fire is real faith (1 Peter 1:7).

Our Savior is the One who walks with us in the fire to bring us through the fire (Daniel 3:25-27).

Jesus baptizes us with His Holy Spirit igniting our souls with His fire (Luke 3:16). Through the Holy Spirit our words are ignited by God's love (Acts 2:3). God's angels minister on holy fire (Hebrews 1:7).

As Paul wrote to Timothy, stir up, kindle afresh, and fan into flame the gracious gift of God's inner fire (2 Timothy 1:6).

"Let us give to God our hearts, all blazing with love, and seek His grace, that the fire may never be quenched." ~ Charles Spurgeon

Remember to stay fired up!

Heavenly Father, thank You for the inner fire that comes from You. Help me to stay fired up for You. When I'm in fiery trials, help me to remember You walk with me in the fire and you will help me walk through. Help my soul to stay burning with Your love so that I may spread Your love.

God's Timeless Truth

"I will bring that group through the fire and make them pure. I will refine them like silver and purify them like gold. They will call on my name, and I will answer them. I will say, 'These are my people,' and they will say, 'The Lord is our God'" (Zechariah 13:9, NLT).

"For You, O God, have proved us; You have tried us as silver is tried, refined, and purified" (Psalm 66:10, AMPC).

"These trials will show that your faith is genuine. It is being tested as fire tests and purifies gold—though your faith is far more precious than mere gold. So, when your faith remains strong through many trials, it will bring you much praise and glory and honor on the day when Jesus Christ is revealed to the whole world" (1 Peter 1:7, NLT).

Jesus "will baptize you with the Holy Spirit and fire" (Luke 3:16c).

"That is why I would remind you to stir up (rekindle the embers of, fan the flame of, and keep burning) the [gracious] gift of God, [the inner fire] ..." (2 Timothy 1:6, AMPC).

Sometimes ya just gotta shake things up

Hints of green played in the top of the trees and early flowering plants blessed with colorful blooms. Spring finally started to show signs of new growth, and I was so ready for a season budding with fresh hope. I had been frazzled and antsy, desperate for answered prayers and to find a balance. While reading Kelly Minter's study, *No Other Gods*, I realized my time on social media was a major problem. Sure, I can tell myself I'm ministering to others, connecting with friends, reading devotions, and encouraging others in ministry.

Even though I hope to do those things, when I'm truly honest with God and myself, I waste more time online than doing anything worthwhile.

God gave me a visual the other morning. Our maple tree sprouts with new growth. Unfortunately, the squirrels found the leaves a tasty temptation, and they did not resist temptation. Our poor tree was looking rather stressed.

A bluebird, nesting in our yard, often knocks on our window to tell us the squirrels are too close for comfort. After taps on the window from our feathered friend, I stepped out on the patio.

A squirrel jumped off the maple tree and ran for cover. Then, another four jumped off the branches and ran. Yikes! If we don't make changes, the poor maple tree might be stripped bare by long-tailed, furry rodents.

In the same way, social media seemed to be stripping bare my time and sanity. I needed to make changes.

God blessed with another squirrel visual. Sweet hubby moved one of our bird feeders to a shepherd crook further back in the yard to try and keep the critters from climbing onto the feeder.

A few minutes after this change, a squirrel climbed up a few feet on the pole and couldn't go further. He returned to the ground to study and analyze the situation. Not to be dissuaded, he again climbed up the pole about a foot, then shook his body. The quaking of the pole caused some of the feeder's content to scatter on the ground. He jumped down, then happily munched on what had fallen. Squirrels are clever little things, aren't they?

Like the squirrel that shook the pole, sometimes we have to shake things up to get the good stuff. I too need to shake things up for my spiritual, emotional, and physical health. I need to chase away things that chase me away from God.

I need to spend time with God without running to immediately post what I'm reading, writing, or learning. Instead, I need to wait for the Holy Spirit's prompting to share.

I'm shaking things up; I'm chasing away things that strip bare my soul and chase me away from God, and I'm relaxing into the strong arms of my Savior, Jesus Christ.

In your spiritual walk, what do you need to shake up? What do you need to chase away?

Heavenly Father, please forgive me for being so distracted. Help me to use my time better and to use social media in a way that honors You. Help me to chase away and throw aside everything that keeps me from running the race You have given me.

Thank You for shaking me up and showing me the things

that have come between us. I ask for Your forgiveness. Thank You that Your kingdom is never shaken. Help me to cease striving and know that You are God.

Thank You, Father for this day. Help me to rejoice and be glad in the days You have given. I love You, Father. I'm resting in You and praising You.

I ask these things in the name of Your Son, Jesus Christ, who is my Savior. Amen.

God's Timeless Truth

"Only the things that cannot be shaken will remain. So, let us be thankful because we have a kingdom that cannot be shaken. We should worship God in a way that pleases him with respect and fear... throw aside every encumbrance (unnecessary weight) and that sin which so readily (deftly and cleverly) clings to and entangles us and let us run with patient endurance and steady and active persistence the appointed course of the race that is set before us" (Hebrews 12:27b-28, NCV, Hebrews 12:1, AMPC).

Joy and true love

Oh, how I want you to find joy and love -- joy and love deeper, wider, more filling than you can imagine. The joy and love you are looking for, longing for, desiring with all your being, is waiting for you. The love you are missing deep in your heart is found in the One who made your heart.

Joy, love, peace, comfort, mercy, forgiveness, are all found in the all-powerful, everlasting, ever-loving God. Love and joy are found in a heart-filling, soul-filling experience with the Savior of the world, Jesus Christ. Perhaps you've heard of Jesus, maybe even used His name, and prayed to His name. Oh, but there is so much more than the name of Jesus.

Jesus is the One who invites you to invite Him into your heart. Jesus will bring your heart to life, wrap your heart in His tender, grace-filled, nail-scarred hands, to give you eternal life full of His everlasting love and joy. The love of Jesus is far better than any human love and any love found on earth. How I long for you to be filled with love that will never let go, joy exceeding anything you could ask or imagine.

Oh, please come home to Jesus. He is the way to true life and eternal joy, peace, and love. Jesus longs to bring you into the eternal safety of His loving embrace.

Come home. The light is always on. The Light of the World is waiting to bring light and life everlasting, peace ever-filling, and joy ever-abounding. Please, come home to joy and true love.

Dear God, please open hearts to Your amazing joy and wonderful, unfailing love. Help them to hear Your call.

Help them to know the love of Christ that is wider, deeper, more incredible than any love on earth. Help them to invite You into their hearts so that they will be filled with Your joy and true love.

God's Timeless Truth

"Look! I stand at the door and knock. If you hear my voice and open the door, I will come in, and we will share a meal together as friends" (Revelation 3:20, NLT).

Oh, how I long for you "to comprehend with all the saints what is the breadth and length and height and depth, and to know the love of Christ which surpasses knowledge, that you may be filled up to all the fullness of God. For I am convinced that neither death, nor life, nor angels, nor principalities, nor things present, nor things to come, nor powers, nor height, nor depth, nor any other created thing, will be able to separate us from the love of God, which is in Christ Jesus our Lord" (Ephesians 3:18-19, Romans 8:38-39, NASB).

Thank You, God. In You, "I experience absolute joy in your presence; you always give me sheer delight" (Psalm 16:11, NET Bible).

Remember the power

I wonder what would happen if we truly understood the power of prayer and the power of praise. Oh, if we only knew, understood, and used the blessings of prayer, praise, and thanksgiving.

> *"Do we know the power of our supernatural weapon? Do we dare to use it with the authority of a faith that commands as well as asks? God baptize us with holy audacity and divine confidence! He is not wanting great men, but He is wanting men who will dare to prove the greatness of their God. But God! But prayer!"*
> *~ A. B. Simpson*

The Psalmist tells us the power of praise and thanksgiving invites us into God's courts (Psalm 100:4-5).

The power of praise defeats the enemy. I love the story about the Israelites who were going into battle. They sent the praise and worship team out front to praise God, and God defeated their enemies (2 Chronicles 20:22).

James tells us that prayer is powerful, dynamic, and effective (James 5:16).

The power of prayer sets the prisoner free. While Peter was in prison, the believers met to pray fervently for his release. And an angel of the Lord came to set Peter free (see Acts 12:5-16).

The power of praise sets the prisoner free, and not only sets free those who are praying and praising, also has a mighty domino effect.

There is GREAT power in praise beyond what we can imagine or conceive.

Paul and Silas were beaten and thrown in prison, and yet they praised God singing hymns and praising. God sent an earthquake, shaking the prison. The doors flew open, and the chains of the prisoners fell off. And then, the jailer and all his household were saved (Acts 16:25-34).

"So many of us limit our praying because we are not reckless in our confidence of God. In the eyes of those who do not know God, it is madness to trust Him, but when we pray in the Holy Ghost, we begin to realize the resources of God, that He is our perfect heavenly Father, and we are His children." ~ Oswald Chambers

Prayer and thanksgiving bring peace. "Do not be anxious or worried about anything, but in everything [every circumstance and situation] by prayer and petition with thanksgiving, continue to make your [specific] requests known to God. And the peace of God [that peace which reassures the heart, that peace] which transcends all understanding, [that peace which] stands guard over your hearts and your minds in Christ Jesus [is yours]" (Philippians 4:6-7, AMP).

Remember the power of prayer. Remember the power of praise. Remember the power of thanksgiving. Remember the power of your all-powerful God.

"Prayer should be the breath of our breathing, the thought of our thinking, the soul of our feeling,

and the life of our living, the sound of our hearing, the growth of our growing. Praying in its magnitude is length without end, width without bounds, height without top, and depth without bottom. Illimitable in its breadth, exhaustless in height, fathomless in depths, and infinite in extension." ~ Homer W. Hodge

Heavenly Father, praise You! Thank You for who You are and all that You do! Thank You for sending Jesus to save us. Thank You for Your grace and mercy.

Thank You that we can come to You and talk with You. Thank You for the incredible blessing of prayer. Help me to remember to come to You to talk with You, listen to You, and spend time with You.

God's Timeless Truth

"Devote yourselves to prayer, keeping alert in it with an attitude of thanksgiving." For, "The eyes of the Lord are toward the righteous and His ears are open to their cry" (Colossians 4:2, Psalm 34:15, NASB).

Therefore, "pray in the Spirit on all occasions with all kinds of prayers and requests..." (Ephesians 6:18, NIV).

"Enter into His gates with thanksgiving, and into His courts with praise. Be thankful to Him and bless His name. For the Lord is good; His mercy is everlasting, and His truth endures to all generations" (Psalm 100:4-5, NKJV).

"The heartfelt and persistent prayer of a righteous man (believer) can accomplish much [when put into action and made effective by God—it is dynamic and can have tremendous power]" (James 5:16, AMP).

New life

The life you've always wanted? I have good news! Jesus didn't come to destroy the life you have or the life you wanted, Jesus came to give you new life, abundant life, joy-filled, love-filled, peace-filled eternal life!

Jesus willingly came to this earth, the God-man Himself, and laid down His life in place of all our sins. Jesus was sinless, yet took on our sins, my sins, your sins, upon His shoulders. He went to the cross as a sacrifice. Jesus died, was buried, and then rose again to give us a life that doesn't end in death.

Jesus Christ gave Himself up for those who will believe in Him so that they could have a restored relationship with God and have eternal life. Jesus is the way, the only way, to God the Father.

There is no greater love, no love like this, that would create heaven and earth, then come from heaven to earth to save His own creation. God's love is a love like no other. God's love calls to you, beckons you, to come to His love. Oh, come to the love of your heavenly Father, come to His Son, Jesus Christ. Open your heart to receive His love, and in return His love will come into your heart to free you forever in His love.

If you want to receive Jesus Christ as Your Savior, would you be willing to pray the following prayer?

Heavenly Father, Thank You for Your grace and mercy. I can never be good enough for heaven, good enough to stand in front of a Holy God. God, I am a sinner, I've messed up, I've failed in many ways.

God, I ask for your forgiveness for my sins. I believe that Your Son, Jesus Christ, died on the cross for my sins and that You raised Him back to life. I want to trust Jesus as Savior of my life. Guide me and help me to follow You. I believe, God. I believe. I pray these things in the name of Jesus Christ who is now my Savior. Amen.

God's Timeless Truth

"**This is how much God loved the world**: He gave his Son, his one and only Son. And this is why: so that no one need be destroyed; by believing in him, anyone can have a whole and lasting life. God didn't go to all the trouble of sending his Son merely to point an accusing finger, telling the world how bad it was. He came to help, to put the world right again. Anyone who trusts in him is acquitted" (John 3:16-17, MSG).

Jesus said, "I am the Door; anyone who enters through Me will be saved [and will live forever], and will go in and out [freely], and find pasture (spiritual security). The thief comes only in order to steal and kill and destroy. **I came that they may have and enjoy life, and have it in abundance [to the full, till it overflows]**" (John 10:9-10, AMP).

"**If you openly declare that Jesus is Lord and believe in your heart that God raised him from the dead, you will be saved**. For it is by believing in your heart that you are made right with God, and it is by openly declaring your faith that you are saved" (Romans 10:9-10, NLT).

For those who come to Christ and make Him Lord of their lives, we have assurance that "**anyone who belongs to Christ has become a new person. The old life is gone; a

new life has begun! And all of this is a gift from God, who brought us back to himself through Christ. And God has given us this task of reconciling people to him" (2 Corinthians 5:17-18, NLT).

"**What a God we have!** And how fortunate we are to have him, this Father of our Master Jesus! **Because Jesus was raised from the dead, we've been given a brand-new life and have everything to live for, including a future in heaven**—and the future starts now! God is keeping careful watch over us and the future. The Day is coming when you'll have it all—**life healed and whole**" (1 Peter 1:3-5, MSG).

So now, dear friend... "**May the God of your hope so fill you with all joy and peace** in believing [through the experience of your faith] that by the power of the Holy Spirit you may **abound and be overflowing (bubbling over) with hope**" (Romans 15:13, AMPC).

(Emphasis added on scripture).

May

Join me in prayer?

Heavenly Father...
May I love You well.
May I always obey You.
May my heart seek You.
May I follow Your truth.
May my heart burn for You.
May I follow Your guidance.
May I always rejoice in You.
May my eyes be focused on You.
May my feet stay on Your path.
May I have a heart of gratitude.
May I enjoy the life You've given me.
May my heart always be open to You.
May my mind be renewed by Your truth.
May nothing and no one come before You.
May I believe You and all You have for me.
May I be on fire to spread Your love and truth.
May I honor You and bring glory to Your name.
May I live in Your love to show others Your love.
May I encourage and build up the body of Christ.
May my ears be tuned to hear You above all others.
May the gifting You have given me be kindled afresh.
May my heart sing your praises for now and forevermore.
May I love You with all my heart, mind, soul, and strength.
May your unfailing love be with us, Lord, even as we put our hope in You.
May the words of my mouth and the meditation of my heart be pleasing to You.

May every beat of my heart, beat with Your love, to show Your amazing love to the world.

May Your glory shine throughout the nations to bring the nations to Your glory.

God's Timeless Truth

"Now may the God who gives endurance and encouragement allow you to live in harmony with one another, according to the command of Christ Jesus, so that you may glorify the God and Father of our Lord Jesus Christ with a united mind and voice" (Romans 15:5-6, HCSB).

"May the Lord of peace Himself give you peace always in every way. The Lord be with all of you" (2 Thessalonians 3:16, HCSB).

"Now may the God of peace Himself sanctify you entirely; and may your spirit and soul and body be preserved complete, without blame at the coming of our Lord Jesus Christ" (1 Thessalonians 5:23, NASB).

About the author

Lisa Buffaloe is a happily married mom, author, and speaker. When she's not writing, she enjoys working in her yard, exploring God's beautiful nature, and taking long walks with her sweet husband.

Lisa loves sharing God's unending love and that through Him we find healing, restoration, renewal, and joy.

Visit Lisa at https://lisabuffaloe.com

Books by Lisa Buffaloe
(Updated July 2023)

Non-Fiction
Float by Faith
Heart and Soul Medication
Time with The Timeless One
The Forgotten Resting Place
Present in His Presence
We Were Meant for Paradise
One Lit Step: Devotions for your journey
The Unnamed Devotional
Flying on His Wings
Unfailing Treasures
No Wound Too Deep for The Deep Love of Christ
Living Joyfully Free Devotional, (Volume 1)
Living Joyfully Free Devotional, (Volume 2)

Fiction
The Masterpiece Beneath
Nadia's Hope (Hope and Grace Series, Book 1)

Prodigal Nights (Hope and Grace Series, 2)
Writing Her Heart (Hope and Grace Series, 3)
The Discovery Chapter (Hope and Grace Series, 4)
Open Lens (Hope and Grace Series, 5)
The Fortune
Grace for the Char-Baked

Acknowledgements

Heavenly Father, thank You for Your unfailing, amazing love. Thank You for blessing us with Your Son, Jesus Christ. Thank You for Your grace and mercy. Thank you for the honor and blessing of writing another book.

Thank you to my sweet family. How grateful I am to be blessed by you.

Kathy McCarthy and Barbara Moore, thank you for the incredible blessing of your time in reading and editing my manuscript. Thank you!

A big thank you to my family, friends (online and in person), and readers. You are all a God-given blessing. Thank you!

Bible credits and Bibliography

The original text of the Bible is rich and full, written in Hebrew, Aramaic, and Greek. The various Bible versions I use during writing are to share the one most appropriate to reveal the beauty and truth of each verse. Some verses are used multiple times to press deep, be cherished, and memorized, the timeless truth of God's word.

I gratefully thank each Bible publisher for the use of the scripture quotations.

Scripture taken from the New Century Version® (NCV). Copyright © 2005 by Thomas Nelson, Inc. Used by permission. All rights reserved.

Living Bible (TLB) The Living Bible copyright © 1971 by Tyndale House Foundation. Used by permission of Tyndale House Publishers Inc., Carol Stream, Illinois 60188. All rights reserved.

Scripture quotations taken from the New American Standard Bible® (NASB), Copyright © 1960, 1962, 1963, 1968, 1971, 1972, 1973, 1975, 1977, 1995 by The Lockman Foundation Used by permission. www.Lockman.org

Scripture quotations marked (NLT) are taken from the Holy Bible, New Living Translation, copyright © 1996, 2004, 2007 by Tyndale House Foundation. Used by permission of Tyndale House Publishers, Inc., Carol Stream, Illinois 60188. All rights reserved.

THE HOLY BIBLE, NEW INTERNATIONAL VERSION®, NIV® Copyright © 1973, 1978, 1984, 2011 by Biblica, Inc.™ Used by permission. All rights reserved worldwide.

NET Bible® copyright ©1996-2006 by Biblical Studies Press, L.L.C. http://netbible.com

Scripture taken from the New King James Version®. Copyright © 1982 by Thomas Nelson, Inc. Used by permission. All rights reserved.

The ESV® Bible (The Holy Bible, English Standard Version®).

ESV® Text Edition: 2016. Copyright © 2001 by Crossway, a publishing ministry of Good News Publishers. The ESV® text has been reproduced in cooperation with and by permission of Good News Publishers. Unauthorized reproduction of this publication is prohibited. All rights reserved.

Scripture taken from *The Message*. Copyright © 1993, 1994, 1995, 1996, 2000, 2001, 2002. Used by permission of NavPress Publishing Group.

Scripture quotations taken from the New Life Version (NLV) Copyright © 1969-2003 by Christian Literature International, P.O. Box 777, Canby, OR 97013. Used by permission.

Scripture quotations taken from the Amplified® Bible (AMP), Copyright © 2015 by The Lockman Foundation Used by permission. www.Lockman.org

Scripture quotations taken from the Amplified® Bible (AMPC), Copyright © 1954, 1958, 1962, 1964, 1965, 1987 by The Lockman Foundation Used by permission. www.Lockman.org

Holman Christian Standard Bible (HCSB) Copyright © 1999, 2000, 2002, 2003, 2009 by Holman Bible Publishers, Nashville Tennessee. All rights reserved.

---

[i] Henry & Richard Blackaby, *Truths from Experiencing God*, LifeWay Press, Nashville, TN, p 14

[ii] Charles H. Spurgeon, *Pictures from Pilgrim's Progress* (Pasadena, TX: Pilgrim, 1992), 87-89

[iii] Blackaby, Henry and Richard Blackaby, Claude King, *Experiencing God, Tennessee:* B & H Publishing, 2007

[iv] Gwen Smith, *I Want It All*, (Colorado Springs: David. C. Cook, 2016)

[v] *Henry & Richard Blackaby, Claude King, Experiencing God*

[vi] *Andrew Murray, Absolute Surrender*

Thank you for reading,

Time with
The Timeless One

Lisa Buffaloe

www.ingramcontent.com/pod-product-compliance
Lightning Source LLC
Chambersburg PA
CBHW061322040426
42444CB00011B/2733